The Case for the Real Jesus

Also by Lee Strobel:

The Case for the Real Jesus
The Case for the Real Jesus (audio)
Finding the Real Jesus
The Case for Christ
The Case for Christ (audio)
The Case for Christ—Student Edition (with Jane Vogel)
The Case for Christ for Kids (with Rob Suggs)
The Case for Christmas
The Case for Christmas (audio)
The Case for a Creator
The Case for a Creator (audio)
The Case for a Creator—Student Edition (with Jane Vogel)
The Case for a Creator for Kids (with Rob Suggs)
The Case for Easter
The Case for Faith
The Case for Faith (audio)
The Case for Faith—Student Edition (with Jane Vogel)
The Case for Faith for Kids (with Rob Suggs)
Discussing the Da Vinci Code (curriculum; with Garry Poole)
Discussing the Da Vinci Code (discussion guide; with Garry Poole)
Experiencing the Passion of Jesus (with Garry Poole)
Exploring the Da Vinci Code (with Garry Poole)
Faith under Fire (curriculum series)
God's Outrageous Claims
Inside the Mind of Unchurched Harry and Mary
Off My Case for Kids (with Robert Elmer)
Surviving a Spiritual Mismatch in Marriage (with Leslie Strobel)
Surviving a Spiritual Mismatch in Marriage (audio)
What Jesus Would Say

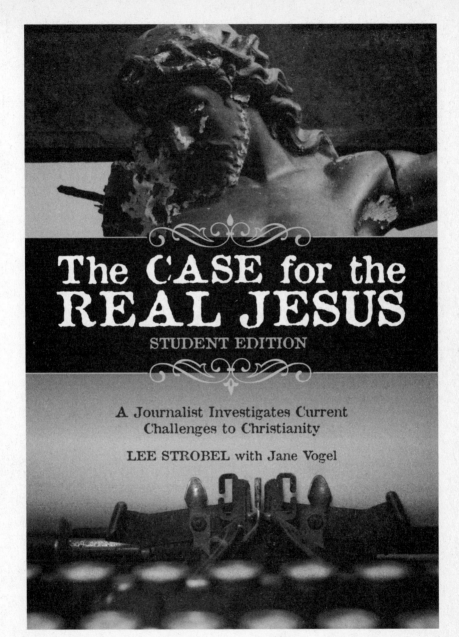

The CASE for the REAL JESUS
STUDENT EDITION

A Journalist Investigates Current
Challenges to Christianity

LEE STROBEL with Jane Vogel

ZONDERVAN.com/
AUTHORTRACKER
follow your favorite authors

youth
specialties

**youth
specialties**

The Case for the Real Jesus—Student Edition
Copyright 2008 by Lee Strobel

Youth Specialties products, 300 S. Pierce St., El Cajon, CA 92020 are published by Zondervan, 5300 Patterson Ave. SE, Grand Rapids, MI 49530.

ISBN 978-0-310-28323-2

Cover design by David Conn
Interior design by Mark Novelli, IMAGO MEDIA

Printed in the United States of America

08 09 10 11 12 • 20 19 18 17 16 15 14 13 12 11 10 9 8 7 6 5 4 3 2 1

CONTENTS

INTRODUCTION

Searching for
the Real Jesus

At first glance, there was nothing unusual about Evergreen Cemetery in Oakland, California. There were the expected rows upon rows of grave markers, some decorated with flowers, others with small American flags. I meandered through the property and soon came upon a gently sloping hillside. Standing sentry over a wide expanse of grass was a solitary three-foot-tall headstone: IN MEMORY OF THE VICTIMS OF THE JONESTOWN TRAGEDY.

Beneath the ground are the remains of more than 400 Californians who followed the call of self-proclaimed messiah Jim Jones to move to the jungles of South America and build a paradise of racial harmony. Believing his creed of love and equal opportunity, beguiled by his charisma, they put their complete faith in Jones.

His boldest claim: He was the reincarnation of Christ—the *real* Jesus.[1]

Jones' followers, intent on living out his doctrine of peace and tolerance, arrived in a remote rainforest of Guyana, only to realize over time that he was building a hellish community of repression and violence. When a visiting U.S. congressman and a group of journalists threatened him with exposure, Jones ordered them ambushed and killed before they could leave on a private plane.

Then Jones issued his now-infamous command: All his followers must drink cyanide-laced punch, and those who refused were shot. Disciples even used syringes to squirt the poison into the mouths of infants. Soon, more than 900 men, women, and children were in the contorted spasms of death under the scorching sun, and Jones ended his own life with a bullet to the head.

The bodies of 409 victims, more than half of them babies and children, were shipped back to California in wooden caskets and buried at Evergreen Cemetery. The Jonestown tragedy happened on November 18, 1978, and since then, few people have visited this section of the cemetery.

On this day, I stood in silence and reverence. As I shook my head at this senseless loss, one thought coursed through my mind: *Beliefs have very real consequences.*

These victims believed in Jones. They subscribed to his utopian vision. His belief became theirs. But the ultimate truth is this: Faith is only as good as the one you believe in.

WHO IS JESUS?

Search for *Jesus* at Amazon.com and you'll find 175,986 books—and, yes, now there's one more (which you're holding). Google Jesus' name and in the blink of an eye, you'll get 165 *million* references. Invite people to tell you who they think the *real* Jesus is—as Jon Meacham and Sally Quinn did at On Faith (a Web site produced by *Newsweek* and *The Washington Post*) just before Christmas in 2006—and you'll soon be buried in an avalanche of wildly differing opinions, as these excerpts demonstrate:

- "Jesus is real, in the sense that he exists for those who want him to exist."

- "By today's standards, Jesus was a liberal."

- "Jesus was Everyman. His name could have as well been Morris. Too bad he was in male form this time around. Better luck next time."

- "I believe Jesus is the Son of God. I believe I am a son of God."

- "Jesus was an enlightened being."

- "It's not even obvious that Jesus was a historical figure. If he was, the legends around him—a Son of God who was born of a virgin, worked miracles, and rose from the dead—were common stories in the ancient Near East. The myths about Jesus are not even original."

- "Jesus is about as 'real' as Santa Claus, the Tooth Fairy, or King Arthur."

- "There is no separation or distinction between where God leaves off and where we begin. We are all One, all Divine, just like Jesus."

- "Jesus was a man we should pity more than revile or worship. He suffered from what contemporary psychologists now know to be delusions of grandeur, bipolar disorder, and probably acute schizophrenia."

- "Jesus is a fairy tale for grown-ups. Unfortunately, he's a fairy tale that leads people to bomb clinics, despise women, denigrate reason, and embrace greed."

- "Who was Jesus? He was an apocalyptic prophet who bet wrong and died as a result. He should be ignored, not celebrated."[2]

As you can see, after two thousand years there's not exactly consensus about the founder of Christianity.

In spite of all this disagreement about Jesus, he's everywhere. I'm not talking about the theological idea of Jesus being spiritually present in all places. I'm talking about pop culture. Here are just a few of the prominent places where Jesus has "appeared" recently:

- *The Da Vinci Code* (novel, 2003; movie, 2006): Jesus as a mortal prophet. This fictional mystery claims that Jesus and Mary Magdalene had children whose descendants are still living today.

- College and university classrooms: Jesus as a legendary character. According to a 2006 study by professors from Harvard and George Mason universities, more than half of college professors believe the Bible is "an ancient book of fables, legends, history, and moral precepts." Less than one-fifth of the general population believes the same.[3]

- *South Park* (airing on Comedy Central since 1992): Jesus as a call-in talk-show host.

All this buzz about Jesus might make you wonder if it's possible to find the *real* Jesus. That depends on how you answer a more foundational question: Are you willing to set aside your preconceptions to let the evidence take you wherever it will? And what about me—am I willing to do the same?

I am. In fact, I had to honestly ask myself that very question when I was an atheist and decided to investigate the identity of Jesus. At the time, I was the legal editor of the *Chicago Tribune*. If you'd asked for my opinion about Jesus back then, I'd have given you a firm answer: If Jesus lived, then he was undoubtedly a rabble-rousing prophet who found himself on the wrong side of the religious and political leaders of his day. I'd ruled out any possibility of the virgin birth, miracles, the resurrection, or anything else supernatural.

It was my agnostic wife's conversion to Christianity and the resulting changes in her character that prompted me to use my legal training and journalism experience to systematically search for the real Jesus. After nearly two years of studying ancient history and archaeology, I found the evidence that led me to the unexpected verdict that Jesus is the unique Son of God who authenticated his divinity by returning from the dead. It wasn't the outcome I was seeking, but I believe it was the conclusion that the evidence persuasively warranted.

For my book *The Case for Christ*, in which I retraced and expanded upon my original journey, I sat down with respected scholars with doctorates from Cambridge, Princeton, Brandeis, the University of Chicago, and elsewhere, peppering them with the tough questions I'd asked as a skeptic. I walked away all the more persuaded that the cumulative evidence established the deity of Jesus in a clear and convincing way.

Not so fast.

That book was published in 1998. Since then the Jesus of historic Christianity has come under increasingly fierce attacks. From college classrooms to best-selling books to the Internet, scholars and popular writers are seeking to debunk the traditional Christ. They're capturing the public's imagination with radical new portraits of Jesus that look very different from the time-honored picture embraced by the Church.

Six specific challenges currently circulating in popular culture are among the most powerful and prevalent objections to Christianity. They've left many Christians scratching their heads and feeling unsure how to respond, and they've confused countless spiritual seekers about who Jesus is—or whether they can come to any solid conclusions about him. Even Christians like me, people who've been convinced for years, have found ourselves troubled by these challenges that threaten to undermine everything we think we know about Jesus Christ.

- Challenge #1: Scholars are uncovering a radically different Jesus through ancient documents just as credible as the four Gospels.

- Challenge #2: The Bible's portrait of Jesus can't be trusted because the church tampered with the text.

- Challenge #3: New explanations have disproved Jesus' resurrection.

- Challenge #4: Christianity's beliefs about Jesus were copied from pagan religions.

- Challenge #5: Jesus was an impostor who failed to fulfill the prophecies about the Messiah.

- Challenge #6: People should be free to pick and choose what to believe about Jesus.

I started hearing these kinds of challenges a few years ago. As someone whose road to faith was paved with painstakingly researched facts and logic, I simply couldn't gloss over these issues. They're too central to the identity of Jesus. I had no choice but to open myself to the possibility they could legitimately unravel the traditional understanding of Christ. For the sake of my own intellectual integrity, I needed answers. And to get them, I needed to hit the road.

My itinerary was already taking shape in my mind: For starters, I'd need to book flights to Nova Scotia and Texas. My goal was to talk to the most credible scholars I could find. I was determined to let the hard evidence of history and the cool demands of reason lead me to a verdict—no matter what it turned out to be.

Yes, I was looking for opinions; but they had to be backed up with convincing data and airtight logic—no speculation, no unquestioned faith. Like the investigations I undertook at the *Chicago Tribune*, I'd have no patience for half-baked claims or unsupported assertions. There was too much hanging in the balance. After all, as Jesus himself cautioned, what you believe about him has very real consequences.[4] And as the Jonestown victims had chillingly reminded me, my faith is only as good as the One I believe in.

This book is your invitation to join me as I retrace the steps of my investigative adventure. We won't need our duffle bags, just open minds and a willingness to follow the facts wherever they take us—even if it's to a conclusion that challenges us on the very deepest levels.

Scholars Are Uncovering a Radically Different Jesus through Ancient Documents Just as Credible as the Four Gospels

The rumor mill was churning. One of my reporters received a tip that police had detained a man running for Illinois governor. The accusation? He'd allegedly abused his wife. If this were true, then the irony would be devastating: One of his responsibilities as the state's chief executive would be to oversee a network of shelters for battered women.

If this politician really had abused his wife, then the voters deserved to know. But before we could responsibly break the story, we needed indisputable confirmation—preferably, a written document—to establish the facts. It would be terrible journalism—not to mention despicable human behavior—to label him an abuser without solid evidence to back up that claim.

The reporters milked their sources. One came up with a timeframe for the incident. Another got the name of the Chicago suburb where the incident allegedly took place in a public parking lot. Still, we didn't have enough. The information was too vague and too unreliable.

Finally, another reporter was able to obtain the key piece of evidence: a police report that described exactly what happened. Because no criminal charges had been filed, privacy laws dictated that all names on the report be blacked out. As the reporter studied the report more carefully, though, she discovered the police had failed to black out the name in one place. Sure enough, it was the candidate's name. Digging deeper in the report yielded the final clue: The suspect had bragged about being the mayor of a certain suburb—the same position held by the candidate. *Bingo!* A match.

In a dramatic confrontation in the *Tribune's* conference room, I peppered the candidate with questions about the incident. He steadfastly denied it ever occurred—until I handed him a copy of the police report. Now faced with the indisputable evidence, he finally admitted to the encounter with police. And within 72 hours, he'd withdrawn from the governor's race.[5]

For both journalists and historians, documents can be invaluable in helping confirm what's happened. Even so, detective work still needs to be done in order to establish the authenticity and credibility of any written record. Questions need to be asked: Who wrote it? Was this person in a position to know what happened? Was he or she motivated by prejudice or bias? Has the document been kept safe from tampering? How legible is it? Is it backed by other external facts? And are there competing documents that might be more reliable or that might shed a whole new light on the matter?

When it comes to understanding the historical Jesus, that last question has become particularly important. For centuries scholars investigating what happened in the life of Jesus relied mostly on the New Testament, especially the books of Mark, Matthew, and Luke—which are the oldest of the four books we call "the Gospels"—as well as the Gospel of John.

In modern times, however, archaeological discoveries have yielded a fascinating crop of other documents from ancient Palestine.

A DIFFERENT JESUS

In the years since my initial investigation into Jesus, the focus on what some scholars call "alternative gospels" has greatly intensified. Both academic and popular books have used these sources to offer a different picture of Jesus. In the 1990s, several participants in the Jesus Seminar (a group of highly liberal and skeptical academics) and others, led by religious studies professor Robert J. Miller, published *The Complete Gospels*, which put the New Testament Gospels side-by-side with 16 other ancient texts.[6]

"Each of these gospel records offers fresh glimpses into the world of Jesus and his followers," says the book.[7] "All of the... texts in this volume are witnesses to early Jesus traditions. All of them contain traditions independent of the New Testament gospels."[8]

THE JESUS SEMINAR

The left-wing Jesus Seminar captivated the media's attention in the 1990s by using colored beads to vote on what Jesus really said. The group's conclusion: Fewer than one in five sayings attributed to Jesus in the Gospels actually came from him. In the Lord's Prayer, the Seminar determined that Jesus said only the words "Our Father." There were similar results when the participants considered which deeds of Jesus were authentic.

What made the Jesus Seminar unique was the way it bypassed the usual academic channels and enthusiastically took its conclusions directly to the public, which was ill-equipped to evaluate them. "These scholars have suddenly become concerned—to the point of being almost evangelistic—with shaping public opinion about Jesus with their research," said one New Testament expert.[9]

A major reason to take these alternative gospels seriously is that some scholars claim they were written as early as the first century, which is when Jesus' ministry flourished and the four Gospels of the New Testament were written. If that's the case, then we can assume they contain very early—and perhaps historically reliable—material.

To me, the implication of this research was clear: These other gospels—with such names as the Gospel of Thomas, the Secret Gospel of Mark, the Gospel of Peter, and the Gospel of Mary—were equal to the biblical accounts in terms of their historical significance and spiritual content. In fact, Philip Jenkins, professor of history and religious studies at Pennsylvania State University, said, "With so many hidden gospels now brought to light, it is now often claimed that the four Gospels were simply four among many of roughly equal worth, and the alternative texts gave just as valid a picture of Jesus as the texts we have today."[10]

The discovery of these other gospels might not be such a big deal if they gave pretty much the same picture of Jesus that the New Testament gives. But some of them paint a very different portrait of Jesus from the one we find in the Bible, and they throw key theological beliefs into question. To see what I mean, Google "Gospel of Thomas." You can find the entire book—a collection of 114 sayings that are attributed to Jesus—online. What you'll read will have some similarities to the New Testament Gospels, but you'll also find some significant differences. Here are a few examples:

SUBJECT	GOSPEL OF THOMAS	NEW TESTAMENT
Who Jesus is	Someone who imparts secret teachings to the disciples who are mature enough to receive it	The Redeemer who saves his people from sin
Salvation	Salvation comes through a special, secret knowledge. You have to be worthy to receive that knowledge.	Salvation comes through faith in Jesus. "And you can't take credit for this; it is a gift from God" (Ephesians 2:8, NLT).
Fasting, prayer, and giving	"If you fast, you will bring sin upon yourselves, and if you pray, you will be condemned, and if you give to charity, you will harm your spirits." (Saying 14)	"When you fast, comb your hair and wash your face" (Matthew 6:17, NLT). "And pray in the Spirit on all occasions with all kinds of prayers and requests" (Ephesians 6:18). "If [your gift] is contributing to the needs of others… give generously" (Romans 12:8).

And that's only one small sampling of one document. Take a look at some of the other alternative gospels:

- The Gospel of Mary: Contrary to the biblical Gospels, this text has Jesus teaching that "salvation is achieved by seeking the true spiritual nature of humanity within oneself and overcoming the entrapping material nature of the body and the world."[11]

- The Secret Gospel of Mark: The most controversial claim in this gospel is that Jesus conducted a secret initiation rite with a young man that, according to one scholar, may have included "physical union."[12]

- The Jesus Papers: Directly contradicting what Christianity has taught for two millennia, Jesus explicitly denies that he's the Son of God, clarifying instead that he only embodies God's spirit as anyone can.[13]

- The Gospel of Judas: The most sensational claims in this text are that Judas Iscariot was Jesus' greatest disciple, that he alone was able to understand Jesus' most profound teaching, and that the two of them conspired to arrange for Jesus' betrayal.

All of this had profound implications for my personal quest to discover the real Jesus. Was it possible my earlier conclusions about him had been unduly colored by New Testament accounts that were really only one perspective among many?

Clearly, a lot was at stake. I needed to have confidence that the *right* people used the *right* reasoning to choose the *right* documents in the ancient world. I needed to know if there was any historical support for these alternative texts that cast Jesus in a different light. I needed to go wherever the evidence took me.

Knowing there are almost as many opinions as there are experts, I wanted to track down someone with sterling credentials, who would be respected by both conservatives *and* liberals, and who, most importantly, could back up any insights with solid facts and reasoning.

That meant flying to Nova Scotia and driving to a quaint village to interview a highly regarded historian. After driving more than an hour from my hotel in Halifax, I ended up in a heavily wooded community near Acadia University. I rang the doorbell at the colonial-style home of Craig A. Evans, professor of New Testament at Acadia.

I believed Evans could help me determine whether these alternative gospels are trustworthy and give me some insight into the way Bible scholars sort out the fact from the fiction.

INTERVIEW #1: CRAIG A. EVANS, PHD

Evans and his wife, Ginny, opened their front door and invited me inside. As we settled into chairs at their dining room table, I decided to start with the question of the legitimacy of the "alternative" gospels.

"With all the alternative gospels coming to light, is there any way to determine whether they are reliable?" I asked as I picked up a homemade chocolate-chip cookie from a tray Ginny had set between us on the table.

Evans thought for a moment. "The best way, I think, is to follow the criteria that historians use in determining whether any ancient document is reliable."

1. When was it written? "The first question is: When was it written?" he said, leaning back in his chair. "If the document is about Alexander the Great, was it written during the lifetime of those who knew him? Same with the New Testament. There's a huge difference between a gospel written in AD 60—about 30 years after Jesus' ministry—and another document written in AD 150.

"If the Gospel of Mark was written in the 60s—some 30 to 35 years after Jesus' ministry—then it was written within the lifetimes of lots of people who would have known Jesus and

Bio: Craig Evans

- Professor of New Testament, Acadia University, 2002 to present
- Professor at Trinity Western University for more than 20 years, where he directed the graduate programs in biblical studies and founded the Dead Sea Scrolls Institute.
- Bachelor's degree in history and philosophy from Claremont McKenna College
- Master of divinity degree from Western Baptist Seminary
- Master's degree and doctorate in biblical studies from Claremont Graduate University (which has produced numerous members of the Jesus Seminar as well)
- Has served as a visiting fellow at Princeton Theological Seminary
- Author or editor of more than 50 books, including *Noncanonical Writings* and *New Testament Interpretation* and *Studying the Historical Jesus*
- Has lectured at Cambridge, Durham, Oxford, Yale, and other universities, as well as the Field Museum in Chicago and the Canadian Museum of Civilization in Ottawa
- Served as editor-in-chief of the *Bulletin for Biblical Research*
- Member of the *Studiorum Novi Testamenti Societas* (SNTS), the Institute for Biblical Research, and the International Organization for Septuagint and Cognate Studies
- Chairman of the Society of Biblical Literature's Scripture in Early Judaism and Christianity Section and the SNTS's Gospels and Rabbinic Literature Seminar
- Has appeared as an expert on numerous television programs, including *Dateline NBC*, and on the History Channel and the BBC

heard him teach. If the gospel writer got it wrong, then people who knew Jesus and his teachings wouldn't accept it. But if a document was written 60, 80, or 100 years later, then that chain is lost. Although it's not impossible that a document written much, much later could contain authentic material, it's a lot more problematic."

2. Where was it written? "A second issue," he said, "involves a geographic connection. For example, a document written in the eastern Mediterranean world 30 years after Jesus' ministry is more promising than one written in Spain or France in the middle of the second century."

3. Does it reflect the culture of the time? "A third issue involves the cultural accuracy of the document, in terms of its allusions to contemporary politics or events. This can expose phony documents that claim to have been written earlier than they really were. When we have a writer in the second or third century who's claiming to be recounting something Jesus did, often he doesn't have the correct details. For example, whoever wrote the so-called Gospel of Peter didn't know Jewish burial traditions, corpse impurity issues, and other matters from Jesus' time. He gets exposed by mistakes he didn't even realize he made."

CHRISTIANITY OR CHRISTIANITIES

At this point, I brought up *The Complete Gospels*. "Some scholars say these other gospels were written very early," I said. "This backs up their claim that first-century Christianity included a broad range of differing doctrines and practices—all equally legitimate—and it was the more powerful orthodox wing that crushed these other valid Christian movements at the council of Nicea in 325. Is it true that the earliest Christianity was a melting pot of all kinds of different perspectives about Jesus?"

The Council of Nicea

In 325, three hundred or so representatives of the Christian church from all over the Roman Empire met in the city of Nicea (now Isnik, Turkey). The result of that conference was the Nicene Creed, the first formal summary statement of what Christians believe. (You can find the Nicene Creed in several places online, if you're interested.)

The disdain was apparent on Evans' face. "It's not true at all," he insisted. "It sounds good today with our emphasis on political correctness, multiculturalism, and sympathy for marginalized groups. It fits in well with the modern attitude that says diversity is always good, truth is negotiable, and every opinion is equally valid. But the question is, what really *did* happen in the first century? What's the evidence? What are the facts?"

I jumped in. "What *are* the facts?" I asked.

"Well, the early Christian movement certainly did have disagreements. But there weren't 'Christianities'—plural. There wasn't one Christianity that thought Jesus was the Messiah and another Christianity that didn't; another Christianity that thought he was divine and another Christianity that disagreed; and another Christianity that thought he died on the cross as a payment for sin and another Christianity that scoffed at that."

"Still," I objected, "we do see the New Testament talking about controversies in the first century, things like whether converts should be circumcised and so forth."

"Yes, and the New Testament quite honestly discusses disagreements when they occur—issues like circumcision, whether Christians can eat meat sacrificed to idols, those kind of tensions," he conceded. "But that's not what these scholars are claiming. They're suggesting that Christians were disagreeing about quite different issues, even though those issues weren't part of first-century Christianity at all."

"So the core message of Christianity...?"

"Is that Jesus is the Messiah, he's God's Son, he fulfills the Scriptures, he died on the cross and thereby saved humanity, he rose from the dead—those core issues were not open for discussion," he said firmly. "If you didn't buy that, then you weren't a Christian."

I wanted to discuss some of the specific alternative gospels, so I decided to start with the Gospel of Thomas, which includes a portrait of Jesus as an imparter of mysterious and secret teachings that has intrigued scholars and captivated the public. The real story behind Thomas, I was soon to learn, was even more fascinating.

DOCUMENT #1: THE GOSPEL OF THOMAS

"History preserves at least a half-dozen references that say there was a gospel purportedly written by Thomas," Evans said in response to my question about the ancient document. "And, by the way, they didn't believe for a minute that this gospel really went back to the disciple Thomas or that it was authentic or early. Nobody was saying, 'Boy, I wish we could find that lost Gospel of Thomas because it's a goodie.' They were saying, 'Somebody cooked this up and it goes by the name of Thomas, but nobody believes that.'"

Hmmmm, I thought to myself. *An interesting start.*

"Then in the 1890s, archaeologists digging in the city dump of ancient Oxyrhynchus, Egypt, found thousands of papyri, including three fragments of the Gospel of Thomas in Greek. Only they didn't know what they were until 1945, when the Nag Hammadi library was discovered at another location in Egypt. Among the documents they found was the Gospel of Thomas in Coptic [an Egyptian language].

"A lot of people assume the Greek version is earlier than the Coptic version. But now the small number of scholars who have competence in the field believe that may not be true. Instead, Thomas was probably written in Syriac. What's particularly interesting is that most of the material in Thomas parallels Matthew, Mark, Luke, John, and sometimes Paul and other sources. Over half the New Testament writings are quoted, paralleled, or alluded to in Thomas."

"What does that tell you?" I asked.

"It tells me it's late," he replied. "For Thomas to quote the New Testament material, obviously that material already had to be in circulation. I'm not aware of a Christian writing before AD

150 that references this much of the New Testament. Go to the Epistles of Ignatius, the bishop of Antioch, which were written around AD 110. Nobody doubts their authenticity. They don't quote even half the New Testament. Then along comes the Gospel of Thomas and it shows familiarity with 14 or 15 of the 27 New Testament writings." His eyebrows shot up. "And people want to date it to the middle of the first century? Come on!"

I interrupted. "Elaine Pagels, professor of religion at Princeton University and author of *Beyond Belief: The Secret Gospel of Thomas*, told me that she dates Thomas' composition to AD 80 or 90, which would be before many scholars date the Bible's Gospel of John. Is it possible that the New Testament Gospels are quoting Thomas instead of the other way around?"

Evans shook his head. "Thomas doesn't have early, pre-Synoptic [that is, prior to Matthew, Mark, and Luke] material. Thomas has forms that reflect the later developments in Luke or Matthew."

I was confused. "Explain what you mean," I said.

"Matthew and Luke sometimes improve on Mark's grammar and word choice. Mark is not real polished in terms of Greek grammar and style, while Matthew and Luke are much more so. And in the Gospel of Thomas we find these more polished Matthew and Luke forms of the sayings of Jesus. So Thomas isn't referring to the earlier Mark, but to the later Matthew and Luke.

"It gets even clearer when we find that some of the material certain scholars think is old and independent actually reflects *Syriac* development."

Again, I asked him to elaborate. "The Gospels are published in the Greek language," he said. "Christianity then spread to all sorts of language groups. Of course it goes eastward, where people speak a form of Aramaic called 'Syriac.'"

"So the Gospels were translated into Syriac?"

"Not immediately. There was a guy named Tatian who in the year 175 blended all four Gospels together into a single book in Syriac. It's called the *Diatessaron*. So the first time Syrian-speaking Christians had access to the Gospels was not as separate Matthew, Mark, Luke, and John, but as the blended, harmonized form.

"In blending together the sayings of the four Gospels, Tatian created some new forms, because it was part Matthew, part Luke, and so forth. Here's the clincher: *Those distinctive Syriac forms show up in the Gospel of Thomas.*

"What's more, a study by Nicholas Perrin has found that, in places, the Gospel of Thomas is also acquainted with the order and arrangement of material in the *Diatessaron*. All this means Thomas must have been written *later* than the *Diatessaron* in 175. Now everything begins to add up. Of course Thomas knows more than half of the New Testament. By the end of the second century, you're in a position to know that much.

"But maybe this is the most interesting evidence," Evans said. "If you read Thomas in Greek or Coptic, it looks like the 114 sayings aren't in any particular order. It seems to be just a random collection of what Jesus supposedly said. But if you translate it into Syriac, something extremely intriguing emerges. Suddenly, you discover more than 500 Syrian catchwords that link virtually all of the 114 sayings in order to help people memorize the gospel.[15] In other words, Saying 2 is followed by Saying 3 because Saying 2 refers to a certain word that's then contained in Saying 3. And Saying 3 has a certain word that leads you into Saying 4. It was a memorization aid.

"So you have distinctive Syrian sayings, you have Syriac catchwords, you have familiarity with more than one-half of the

THOMAS TIMELINE

Jesus was crucified in AD 30 or 33. The Gospel of Mark, first of the New Testament Gospels, was probably written in the late AD 50s or early AD 60s.

The Gospels of Matthew and Luke: Probably written after Mark because they contain some material from Mark, but with more polished grammar and word choices. Matthew, Mark, and Luke are called "synoptic" Gospels (from the Greek words for "seeing together") because all three have a similar viewpoint and share material. Many scholars date Matthew and Luke to the AD 60s.

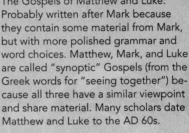

New Testament—what does it all add up to? Everything points to Thomas being written at the end of the second century, no earlier than 175 and probably closer to 200."

I had to admit that Evans had done a persuasive job in establishing that the Gospel of Thomas dates to the late second century and therefore lacks credibility in its depiction of Jesus. However, I was still interested in how this ancient text portrays him. After all, more and more people are exploring Gnosticism, a philosophy reflected in the Gospel of Thomas.

Gnosticism

Gnosticism (the name comes from the Greek word *gnosis*, which means "knowledge") is a mystical religion focusing on experiential knowledge or enlightenment. Although many variations on Gnosticism exist, generally the physical and material world is seen as evil and only the spiritual is good.

"How does Jesus in the Gospel of Thomas differ from the Jesus we see in the four Gospels?" I asked Evans.

The Gospel of John was probably written around AD 90, although some argue for an earlier date.

▶ Tatian wrote the *Diatessaron*—a blending of Mark, Matthew, Luke, and John into a single narrative—in the Syriac language around AD 175.

▶ The Gospel of Thomas includes material from Mark, Matthew, Luke, and John, but it uses some of the form and sequence found in the *Diatessaron*. This means Thomas came later than AD 175, with many scholars dating it close to AD 200.

"Jesus in Thomas teaches a mystical understanding of the Good News," he responded. "That is, inner light, inner revelation, freeing oneself from materialism, greed, and the usual worries of life. Some of the material in Thomas is in step with Wisdom teaching, like the book of Proverbs, and even with some of Jesus' teaching. It's just skewed or exaggerated so it becomes inner, mystical, private, personal, and not very communal or collective.

"There's no longer any interest in this world being redeemed. That, of course, is the Gnostic element. This world is hopeless. It's lost. It will be destroyed, rather than being restored and redeemed. Israel's promises no longer mean anything. In fact, there's a touch of anti-Semitism in Thomas."

"It's a bit anti-women, too, isn't it?" I added.

"Yes, it's very politically incorrect the way it concludes," he said. "Simon Peter says, 'Miryam'—or Mary—'should leave us. Females are not worthy of life,' and Jesus answers, 'Look, I shall guide her to make her male, so she too may become a living spirit resembling you males. For every female who makes herself male will enter the kingdom of heaven.'"

Interestingly, the Gnostic Gospels as a whole don't elevate women in the way some authors have claimed. As Ben Witherington III of Asbury Theological Seminary points out:

> The Gnostic literature is written by those who wish to get beyond human sexual matters, who see such material things as hindrances to the core of a person's true identity. Thus it is not true that women are more affirmed as women in the Gnostic literature than they are in the canonical Gospels. Quite the opposite is the case. The Gnostic literature is all about transcending or ignoring one's material or bodily identity. But the canonical Gospels affirm maleness and femaleness as part of the goodness of God's creation.[16]

"What about salvation in Thomas?" I asked Evans.

"Salvation is not perhaps exactly the way it is in other Gnostic texts, but it's pretty close," he answered. "It comes from self-knowledge, from understanding oneself authentically, and from recognizing where one fits into the cosmos, as well as repudiating and not getting caught up with this world. So it's slightly Christian, slightly Old Testament, slightly Gnostic."

"And the resurrection?"

He leaned forward. "That's an interesting question," he said. "Jesus is called the 'living one.' Some wonder if the post-Easter and pre-Easter Jesus are blended together in Thomas. But it doesn't even matter to them—this is the *revealing* Jesus."

"History itself doesn't seem to matter very much to the Gnostics," I observed.

"Yes, that's right," Evans said. "Contrast that with the New

Testament Gospels. The reason for the Christian movement in the New Testament is that an event of history has taken place. Jesus has become flesh, we have seen him, we have touched him, he died on the cross, and on Sunday morning he was resurrected. But for the Gnostics, Jesus is a revealer—he tells us things and we must internalize and live in light of them. What actually happened becomes less relevant. It isn't the story that counts anymore; it's the thought. It isn't a response of faith in something God has done; it's just knowing what you're supposed to know."

"So the idea of Jesus dying for our sins would not be a..." I said, pausing to let him finish the sentence.

"No, in their view Jesus didn't die for our sins," he said. "He came so that we would have knowledge. How he left doesn't matter."

I decided to ask his opinion about something else Pagels had said to me—suspecting he would again be direct in his answer.

"Pagels thinks the Gospel of Thomas should be read alongside Mark, which is the public teaching of Jesus, because Thomas 'possibly' preserves Jesus' private teaching," I said. "Would you suggest people use Thomas in this way?"

"I disagree profoundly," came his immediate response. "That's wishful thinking. I don't think there's any hope in the world that this is Jesus' private teaching. Let's put it this way: If anything in the Gospel of Thomas actually goes back to Jesus, it's because it reflects authentic tradition that is already preserved in Matthew, Mark, Luke, and John. Everything distinctive in Thomas turns out to be late second-century Syrian tradition."

Referring to my notes, I read Evans this quote from Philip Jenkins:

> The new portrait of Gnosticism is profoundly attractive for modern seekers, that large constituency interested in spirituality without the trappings of organized religion or dogma. For such an audience, texts like Thomas are so enticing because of their individualistic quality, their portrait of a Jesus who is a wisdom teacher rather than a Redeemer or heavenly Savior.[17]

"Do you think that's true?" I asked.

"We're seeing an increased interest in spirituality and a decreased interest in organized religion," he said. "Well, that makes Thomas attractive. If you don't care about history or what really occurred with Jesus, if you're not interested in the organized church, then Thomas would be interesting. And Thomas doesn't lay very heavy demands on anyone. You're chastised for being ignorant—well, nobody wants to be ignorant. [Yet,] there isn't any severe rebuke for immorality or injustice—things the authentic Jesus *does* talk about."

My thoughts went to people who are reading exaggerated claims about Thomas in books and on the Internet. "What about average, everyday Christians?" I said. "What current value does Thomas have for them?"

Evans thought for a moment before answering. "I don't know that Thomas has any value for everyday Christians. If you're looking for the real Jesus, there are far, far better places to go—like the New Testament Gospels," he said. "However, I tell my students that if they're curious about documents outside the New Testament, then go ahead and read them. I say,

'You tell me: Should Thomas be right alongside Matthew, Mark, Luke, and John?' Without exception, they come back and say, 'My goodness, what weird stuff. Good grief! Now I think the church chose wisely.'"

DOCUMENT #2: THE GOSPEL OF MARY

Popularized by Dan Brown's novel *The Da Vinci Code*, the Gospel of Mary has become increasingly fashionable, especially among women who see it as validating female leadership in the church.

"What about any historical connection with Mary herself?" I asked Evans.

"Nobody in all seriousness—who's a scholar and is competent—would say Mary Magdalene composed this gospel that now bears her name."

"Her name was attached to legitimize it?" I asked.

"Sure. And by the way, that's what Gnostics would do. In contrast, the Gospels of Matthew, Mark, and Luke circulated anonymously. Their authority and truth were transparent. Everybody knew this was what Jesus taught, so there wasn't much concern over who wrote it down. But in the second century, they had to force it. So the [writers of the alternative] gospels of the second century and later would attach a first-century name to try to boost their credibility, since [the writings] didn't sound like Jesus. They had to compensate by saying, 'Well, Thomas or Peter or Philip or Mary wrote it, so it *must* have credibility.'"

"You'd date the Gospel of Mary to the second century?"

"Yes, probably between 150 and 200," he replied. "And, frankly, that's not very controversial. Scholars are virtually unanimous about this. There's nothing in it that we can trace back with any confidence to the first century or to the historical Jesus or to the historical Mary."[18]

"I hesitate to bring this up, because it's already been thoroughly debunked by so many credible scholars," I said, "but we might as well mention that this gospel does not actually support the now-popular idea that Jesus was married to Mary."

"No legitimate scholar believes they were wed," he replied. "That idea might make for page-turning fiction, but only the truly gullible—or those advancing their own theological agenda—buy into that."

DOCUMENT #3: THE SECRET GOSPEL OF MARK

I've investigated lots of extraordinary cases as a journalist: police framing innocent people, corporate bigwigs knowingly producing dangerous products, and politicians engaging in corruption of all kinds. But as I sat in the Evanses' dining room, listening in astonishment, Dr. Evans unfolded a bizarre story of academic intrigue that rivaled anything I'd ever landed on the front page of the *Chicago Tribune*. On the surface, the Secret Gospel of Mark's homoerotic suggestions were shocking enough; but beneath the surface, the story behind the gospel left me shaking my head in bewilderment.

"The story goes like this," Evans began. "Morton Smith was a professor at Columbia University for years. At a meeting of the Society of Biblical Literature in 1960, he announced that two years earlier he'd made a historic discovery at the Mar Saba Monastery in the Judean wilderness.

"In the back of a 1646 book were two and a half pages of a

letter ostensibly from Clement of Alexandria, who lived in the second century, to someone named Theodore. Smith speculated that a monk copied the letter onto the blank pages at the back of the book to preserve it, maybe because the original papyrus had been crumbling.

"The letter was in Greek, and Smith said it was written with an eighteenth-century hand. Here's what's so interesting: The letter contained two quotes from a previously unknown mystical or secret version of the Gospel of Mark. It describes Jesus raising a young man from the dead, and then later the youth comes to him 'wearing a linen cloth over his naked body' and 'remained with him that night' so he could be taught 'the mystery of the kingdom of God.' Frankly, the homoerotic suggestion was hard to miss. The letter then ends very abruptly, just after it indicates that something really important was going to be revealed."

"How important was this discovery?" I asked.

"Well, if it really was written by the author of the Gospel of Mark, then it would certainly be significant," Evans said. "Smith later wrote two books analyzing it—one 450-page scholarly treatment published by Harvard University Press, and a more popular edition for a general audience. A few prominent scholars from the Jesus Seminar said Clement's letter could contain an earlier version of Mark than what we have in the New Testament. They made some pretty bold claims about it. But from the beginning, there were rumblings that this might be a forgery."

Indeed, the headlines in the *New York Times* at the time of Smith's announcement reflected the brewing controversy. "A New Gospel Ascribed to Mark," said the newspaper on December 30, 1960. The next day came this headline: "Expert Disputes 'Secret Gospel.'"

For a journalist, the next question was obvious: "Why wasn't the document simply examined by experts?"

"Because," Evans said with a grin, "it's gone. *Vanished*. Smith said he left it at the monastery; but nobody can find it, so it can't be subjected to ink tests and other analyses. He did photograph it, and after he died in 1991, large color photographs of the text were studied by Stephen Carlson."

Carlson, a well-regarded patent attorney and amateur biblical scholar, thoroughly investigated the case, bringing in handwriting experts and then writing *The Gospel Hoax: Morton Smith's Invention of Secret Mark* in 2005.[19]

"What's your opinion about the authenticity of the letter?" I asked.

Evans' answer was dramatic: "I think the clues clearly lead to the conclusion that the letter is a hoax and that Smith is almost certainly the hoaxer."

I sat back in my chair. This was absolutely incredible to contemplate: a prominent professor supposedly falsifying an ancient letter and fooling a lot of other scholars who formulated their own elaborate theories based on the spurious text.

"What does it say about biblical scholarship," I asked Evans, "that many scholars apparently accepted Secret Mark without asking enough critical questions?"

"I think it's an embarrassment," came his reply. "Too many well-publicized scholars are so fond of oddball documents and theories that they were too ready to accept Secret Mark as genuine. In fact, some in the Jesus Seminar were too quick to say, 'Well, yes, there probably was a Secret Mark floating around' and 'Well, yes, it probably is earlier than the canonical Mark.'

"And Smith," he added, "had to be laughing."

DOCUMENT #4: THE JESUS PAPERS

I knew I was going to get an earful when I brought up Michael Baigent's recent bestseller *The Jesus Papers*. Baigent reports the discovery of two papyrus documents, both written in Aramaic and dated back to the time of Jesus' crucifixion. Scholars uniformly scoff at Baigent's conspiracy theories and poorly supported allegations, which may sound convincing to those untrained in ancient history, but which quickly collapse upon further examination by experts. Baigent, also the coauthor of *Holy Blood, Holy Grail*, isn't a historian; his degrees are in psychology and "mysticism and religious experience." Still, I couldn't ignore a book that has received as much media attention—and sold as many copies—as *The Jesus Papers*.

"If we were to find something that we had good reason to believe Jesus actually composed, then that would be breathtaking," Evans said. "But the flimsiness of this entire thing is just ridiculous. Baigent says he met somebody who said that in 1961, while excavating underneath a house in Jerusalem, he found two documents written in Aramaic, which he showed to two famous archaeologists who confirmed their date and authenticity. They dated them to roughly the time that Jesus was put to death.

"Baigent describes how he went into a walk-in safe of an antiquities collector and saw the papyri under glass. He couldn't take a picture of them, of course. He's since admitted he doesn't read Aramaic and the other guy doesn't either—so how does he know what they say? He's assured us that two well-known archaeologists, Yigael Yadin and Nahman Avigad, confirmed it. Oh, but did I mention that Yadin and Avigad are dead?

"So we have an author with dubious credibility; an antiquities dealer who can't be identified; documents that Baigent can't read or produce and for which we have no translation or verification; and two archaeologists who are dead. This is just the dumbest thing."

"Yet," I pointed out, "the book became a bestseller and some people apparently believe it."

"It's astounding," he said, his voice betraying more frustration than amazement. "It's possible that there are some documents under glass. But there's not much likelihood that they're ancient. No papyrus buried in the ground in Jerusalem will survive 2,000 years, period. This might happen in the dry sands of the Dead Sea region or Egypt, but it rains in Jerusalem. It's nothing to get two inches of snow during January in Jerusalem. You can't bury papyrus in the moist ground and expect it to still be there—and be legible—two thousand years later. Any archaeologist will tell you that. So there's nothing to this.

"He's playing on the ignorance of people, as well as the desire for a titillating tale of conspiracy, intrigue, and hiding the truth."

DOCUMENT #5: THE GOSPEL OF JUDAS

On April 6, 2006, facing the bright television lights of more than a hundred members of the news media, Evans was among the group of biblical scholars who announced the discovery and translation of the long-lost Gospel of Judas. The National Geographic Society had recruited Evans to be part of a team to assist with interpreting the ancient manuscript, which was discovered in the late 1970s and took a circuitous route to end up the focus of intense worldwide interest.

Carbon-14 dating indicates the papyrus dates back to AD 220 to 340, although team members leaned toward 300 and

320. The original gospel, however, was written prior to 180, which is when the church father Irenaeus warned that this "fictitious history" was floating around.[20]

I said to Evans, "You and the other scholars involved with this project have been careful to caution that this gospel doesn't really tell us anything reliable about Jesus or Judas. But I've seen all kinds of wild speculation about it on the Internet. Does that concern you?"

"When we announced the discovery, I speculated that some popular writers would produce fanciful tales about the 'true story' behind this gospel—and apparently that's happening to some extent," he answered. "Unfortunately, it's a reflection of what we've seen with some of these other gospels. Just because something appears on a screen or in a book, that doesn't mean it's true. I'd caution people to apply the historical tests I mentioned earlier [dating, authorship, and cultural accuracy] and then make a reasoned judgment instead of being influenced by irresponsible conspiracy theories and other historical nonsense."

TESTING THE BIBLE'S FOUR GOSPELS

I took a moment to assess how far we'd come. I'd started with the question of whether these "alternative" gospels could tell me anything new about the real Jesus. Contrary to the claims of a few far-left scholars, however, all of them failed the tests of historicity. The Gospel of Thomas could tell me something about second-century mysticism and Gnosticism, but nothing about Jesus beyond a few quotations lifted from the New Testament. The Gospels of Mary and Judas were written too late to be meaningful. The Secret Gospel of Mark is a hoax, and *The Jesus Papers* are a joke.

All of this brought me back to Matthew, Mark, Luke, and John. How would they fare when subjected to a historian's scrutiny? I asked Evans what he considered to be the best criteria for assessing their reliability.

"One criterion historians use is 'multiple attestation,'" he replied. "In other words, when two or three of the Gospels are saying the same thing, independently—as they often do—then this significantly shifts the burden of proof onto somebody who says they're just making it up. There's also the criterion of 'coherence.' Are the Gospels consistent with what we know about the history and culture of Palestine in the 20s and 30s? Actually, they're loaded with details that we've determined are correct, thanks to archaeological discoveries.

"Then there's the dating issue. Matthew, Mark, and Luke were written within a generation of Jesus' ministry; John is within two generations. That encourages us to see them as reliable because they're written too close to the events to get away with a bunch of lies."

Seeking to clarify a key issue, I said: "When you say Mark was written within a generation of Jesus' ministry, you're not suggesting the author had to think back and remember something that happened more than three decades earlier."

"No, there's no one individual who had to try to remember everything. We're not talking about the story of Jesus being remembered by one or two or three people who never see each other. We're talking about whole communities, never smaller than dozens and probably in the hundreds—lots of people pooling and sharing their stories. People were meeting frequently, reviewing Jesus' teaching, and making it normative for the way they lived. The teaching was being called to mind and talked about all the time."

"So your assessment of the Gospels' reliability is—what?"

"I would say the Gospels are essentially reliable, and there are lots and lots of other scholars who agree. There's every reason to conclude that the Gospels have fairly and accurately reported the essential elements of Jesus' teachings, life, death, and resurrection. They're early enough, they're rooted into the right streams that go back to Jesus and the original people, there's continuity, there's proximity, there's verification of certain distinct points with archaeology and other documents, and then there's the inner logic. That's what pulls it all together."

"What about the argument that the Gospels are inherently unreliable because they're basically faith documents written to convince people of something?"

"In other words, if you have a motive for writing, then it's suspect?" he asked. "There's always a purpose behind anything that's written. Faith and truthful history aren't necessarily at odds."

I issued another challenge. "The Gospels report Jesus doing miraculous things," I said. "To the twenty-first-century mind, doesn't this lead to the conclusion that these writings lack credibility?"

"I say let historians be historians. Look at the sources. They tell us that people in antiquity observed that Jesus could do things far better, far more effectively, far more astoundingly than the scribes could in dealing with healings and exorcisms. In their mind, there was only one way to explain it—it's a miracle. For us to come along and say, 'Unless we can explain it scientifically, metaphysically, and philosophically, we should just reject it,' is high-handed arrogance. Bruce Chilton of Bard College says it's enough for the historian to simply say that the documents tell us this is the way Jesus was perceived by his contemporaries."

"How about the claim we see in *The Da Vinci Code* that Constantine collated the books of the Bible in the fourth century and burned all the alternative gospels?"

"That's just nonsense," he said. "The idea of Constantine telling Christians what ought to be in the Bible and gathering up gospels and burning them—that's fictional material in Dan Brown's book. It isn't legitimate history written by historians who know what they're talking about."

THE IDENTITY OF JESUS

"There's no question in my mind that Jesus understood himself as being the figure described in Daniel 7[21] and that he was anointed to proclaim the Good News—the rule of God," Evans stated. "He is Israel's Messiah as he defines it, but not as others did. Others saw the Son of David as coming to kill Romans, including the emperor. That was the popular view. Jesus then shocks everyone by saying, no, he actually wants to extend messianic blessing—even to the Gentiles.

"So we're on very, very solid footing that Jesus has a messianic self-understanding. But, again, that means more than the fact that he was anointed. Any prophet or priest could claim that. No, the anointing is more than that—there's a divine sense. *He is God's Son.*

"That's the importance of the parable of the wicked vineyard tenants. In that story, told by Jesus, the vineyard owner leased his place to tenant farmers. But when the landowner would send servant after servant to collect his share, the tenants would beat or kill them. Finally, the owner sends his 'beloved son,' and they kill him, too. When the parable is interpreted in its context, we see that the vineyard owner is God, the tenants represent ancient Israel, and the servants represent prophets. The point is clear: God sent his Son. Otherwise, Jesus would just be one more messenger, one more prophet. No—now God has sent his Son, and that's Jesus himself."

DEITY *AND* HUMANITY

I intended to wrap up our interview by asking Evans to expand upon his own personal convictions. I anticipated he'd further elaborate on the divinity of Jesus—and yet our discussion ended with an unexpected turn.

"How have your decades of research into the Old and New Testaments affected your personal view of Jesus?" I asked.

"Well, it's much more nuanced. But at the end of the day, it's a more realistic Jesus. Personally, I think a lot of Christians—even conservative Christians—are semi-Docetic."

That took me off guard. "What do you mean?"

"In other words," he said, "they halfway believe—without ever giving it any serious thought—what the Docetic Gnostics believed, which is that Jesus wasn't actually real. 'Oh, yes, of course he's real,' they'll say. But they're not entirely sure how far to go with the incarnation. How *human* was Jesus? For a lot of them, the human side of Jesus is superficial.

"It's almost as though a lot of Christians think of Jesus as God wearing a human mask. He's sort of faking it, pretending to be human. He pretends to perspire, and his stomach only appears to gurgle because, of course, he's not really hungry. In fact, he doesn't really need to eat. So Jesus is the bionic Son of God who isn't really human.

"But the divine nature of Jesus should never militate against his full humanity. When that part gets lost, you end up with a pretty superficial understanding of Christology. For example, could Jesus read? People want to say, 'Of course he could read! He's the Son of God!' But that's not a good answer. At the age of three days, was Jesus fluent in Hebrew? Could he do quantum physics? Well, then, why does the book of Hebrews talk about him learning and so forth?"

I was listening intently. "What is it we miss about his humanity?" I asked.

"Well, a big part of the atonement. Jesus dies in our place as a human being who dies in our place. God didn't send an angel," he replied. "And, of course, there's the identification factor. We can identify with him: Jesus was tempted as we are. How was he tempted if he were just God wearing a mask— faking it and pretending to be a human?"

"Is there something about his human nature that you'd want to emphasize?"

Evans reflected for a moment, then replied. "Yes, Jesus' own faith," he said. "He tells his disciples to have faith. Jesus has a huge amount of credibility if we see him as fully human and he actually, as a human, has faith in God. Otherwise, well, that's easy for him to say! Good grief—he's been in heaven, and now he's walking around telling *me* to have faith? But I take the teaching of Jesus' humanness, which is taught clearly in Scripture, very seriously."

"Taking everything into consideration," I said, wrapping up our discussion, "when you think about the identity of the real Jesus, where do you come down?"

"I come down on the side of the church," he said. "Doggone it, bless their bones, I think they figured it out. They avoided errors and pitfalls to the left and to the right. I think the church got it right. Even if you consider only the Gospels of Matthew, Mark, and Luke, you find that Jesus saw himself in a relationship with God that's unique. The Son of God is the way that's understood. And then he goes further and demonstrates that he was speaking accurately. If you have any doubts, the Easter event should remove them.

"That's where you always wind up: the Easter event. Otherwise, you have a Moses-like or Elijah-like figure who's able to do astonishing miracles—but so what? Yet the resurrection confirmed who Jesus was. And the resurrection is, of course, very powerfully attested because you have all classes—men and women, believers, skeptics, and opponents—who encounter the risen Christ and believe in him."

He looked me straight in the eyes. "As I do."

The Bible's Portrait of Jesus Can't Be Trusted Because the Church Tampered with the Text

When I was a reporter at the *Chicago Tribune*, a college student from a small Midwestern town was hired as a summer intern. Her parents were nervous about her working in such a big and volatile city, so her mother regularly called to check up on her.

One day the phone rang on the intern's desk, and a passing reporter picked up the phone. When the intern's mother asked if she could speak to her daughter, the reporter replied: "Oh, I'm sorry—she's in the morgue."

The shriek through the phone line instantly sensitized the reporter to the fact that not everyone was familiar with newspaper jargon. He wasn't referring to the county morgue, where dead bodies are temporarily stored and autopsied; in journalism lingo, the "morgue" is the newspaper library where old articles are filed.

The term *morgue* is still in use today, but technology has radically transformed how newspapers deal with their archives. Most historians today don't get to handle the original newspaper clippings on yellowing and brittle newsprint. Instead, they get an electronic version of the story—one that easily could have been altered by someone intent on rewriting history.

For example, during the Watergate investigation in the 1970s, the *New York Times*, to its unending embarrassment, was repeatedly scooped by its rival, the *Washington Post*. What if someone in the *Times'* library simply went into the texts of some Watergate articles and changed them to make it appear as though the *Times* had actually beaten the *Post* to the punch?

That's not so different from the next question I needed to answer. We don't have an original text of the New Testament, as the earliest papyrus copies were reduced to dust long ago. And up until the first Greek New Testament was produced on a printing press in the early sixteenth century, scribes would make handwritten copies of New Testament manuscripts. Errors were inevitable in this very human process, so how can we be sure the text we have today hasn't been altered in significant ways?

AN UNRELIABLE SOURCE?

A lot of people began asking that question when Bart D. Ehrman's book *Misquoting Jesus* exploded onto the best sellers list in 2006. For months, it was the top religion book in America. Actually, the book's title is a misnomer. There's almost nothing in its 242 pages about the words of Jesus having been misquoted. (Reportedly, Ehrman wanted to name the book *Lost in Transmission*, but the publisher thought that made it sound like an automotive book.) The book's underlying message, however, was that readers can't really trust the text of their Bibles. It follows, then, that the common portrait of Jesus that's gleaned from the New Testament might not be reliable after all.

Ehrman can't be dismissed as an academic slouch. He received his master's degree and doctorate from Princeton Theological Seminary, and he's currently the chairman of the Department of Religious Studies at the University of North Carolina at Chapel Hill. He's also written or contributed to 19 books.

"How does it help us to say that the Bible is the inerrant word of God if in fact we don't have the words that God inerrantly inspired, but only the words copied by the scribes—sometimes correctly but sometimes (many times!) incorrectly?" Ehrman asked. "We don't have the originals! We have only error-ridden copies, and the vast majority of these are centuries removed from the originals and different from them, evidently, in thousands of ways."[22]

The issues Ehrman raises in his book are now challenging the faith of many Christians. Here's the text of an e-mail I received:

> Please help me. I have just read Bart Ehrman's book *Misquoting Jesus.* I was raised in the church, and I'm now 26 years old. This book has devastated my faith. I don't want to be kept in the dark; I want to know what really is going on in the Bible and what I should believe, even if it goes against what I've believed since I was a little boy. *Is Ehrman correct?*

That's the question that prompted me to jump on a jet headed for Dallas to seek out another renowned scholar whose credentials rival Ehrman's. At stake was nothing less than whether the New Testament can be trusted to provide a reliable picture of the real Jesus.

INTERVIEW #2: DANIEL B. WALLACE, PHD

Chilling escapes from death, amazing coincidences, weird twists of fate, oddball occurrences—sooner or later, all reporters get pressed by their editors into writing a short item about some sort of wacky circumstance that belongs in *Ripley's Believe It or Not*. I've covered my share through the years. People read them with wide eyes, then put down the paper and exclaim, "Wow, that's really strange!" These are the types of articles that get forwarded all around the Internet.

Daniel B. Wallace could be one of those stories. How's this for bizarre: Wallace, though he hardly knew the Greek language, taught himself this ancient language and became one of the world's leading experts in ancient Greek—and he did it by studying the textbooks that *he'd written!*

Okay, that calls for an explanation. Wallace is famous among seminarians for his textbook *Greek Grammar beyond the Basics*, which is used by more than two-thirds of the schools that teach intermediate Greek, including Yale Divinity School, Princeton Theological Seminary, and Cambridge University.

After Wallace completed this textbook, a crippling bout of viral encephalitis confined him to a wheelchair for more than a year and wreaked havoc with his memory. At one point, he even had difficulty remembering his wife's name. Eventually, he lost his knowledge of

Bio: Daniel Wallace

- Professor of New Testament Studies at Dallas Theological Seminary
- Postdoctoral study at Tyndale House, Cambridge, as well as at Tübingen University and the *Institut für Neutestamentliche Textforschung*, both in Germany
- Executive director of the Center for the Study of New Testament Manuscripts, whose objective is to digitally preserve New Testament manuscripts so scholars and others can examine them via enhancement software on the Internet[24]
- Senior New Testament editor of the New English Translation of the Bible (NET)
- Member of the prestigious *Studiorum Novi Testamenti Societas* (SNTS)
- Author of articles for *New Testament Studies, Novum Testamentum, Biblica, Westminster Theological Journal,* and the *Bulletin for Biblical Research, Nelson's Illustrated Bible Dictionary,* and the Biblical Studies Foundation Web site[25]
- Coauthor of several books, including *Reinventing Jesus*

Greek almost completely, which is what prompted him to use his own book and others to relearn the difficult language.

In the world of textual critics—scholars who try to determine the original text of the Bible—Wallace's name is one of the few that can be appropriately uttered alongside Ehrman's. That's what brought me knocking on the door of his suburban Dallas home one Friday evening, which happens to be pizza night in the Wallace household. We sat around his kitchen table, enjoying dinner and casual conversation, and then we adjourned to his office, a two-story, dark wood library with a capacity of 6,000 books.

Wallace is a fascinating mix of California kid and revered academic. He's a former surfer who once prowled the churning waters off Newport Beach and who now relishes the countless hours he spends in austere monasteries and dusty libraries. He travels Europe and the Middle East, painstakingly photographing ancient manuscripts to preserve them for scholars.

INSPIRATION, INERRANCY, INFALLIBILITY

I wanted to get some definitions straight at the outset. "The Bible says that all Scripture is 'divinely inspired,' that is, 'God-breathed,'"[26] I said. "Exactly what do Christians believe was the process by which God created the New Testament?"

"We aren't given a lot regarding the process of inspiration, but we know the Bible wasn't dictated by God," Wallace replied. "Look at the Old Testament: Isaiah has a huge vocabulary and is often considered the Shakespeare of the Hebrew prophets, while Amos was a simple farmer with a much more modest vocabulary. Yet both books were inspired. Obviously, this doesn't mean verbal dictation. God wasn't looking for stenographers but holy people to write his book."

"Then how does inspiration work?" I asked.

"We get some clues when Matthew quotes the Old Testament, saying, 'This was spoken by the Lord through the prophet.'[27] 'By the Lord' suggests God is the source of that prophecy. 'Through the prophet' suggests an intermediate agent who also uses his personality. That means this prophet was not taking dictation from God; instead, God was communicating through visions, dreams, and so forth, and the prophet was putting it in his own words. So the process doesn't bypass the human personality, yet ultimately the result is exactly what God wanted to produce."

Seeking a crisp summary, I said, "Complete this sentence: When Christians say the Bible is *inspired*, they mean..."

"That it's both the Word of God and the words of men. Lewis Sperry Chafer put it well: 'Without violating the authors' personalities, they wrote with their own feelings, literary abilities, and concerns. But in the end, God could say, 'That's exactly what I wanted to have written.'"

Wallace stopped for a moment, apparently pondering whether to offer one more remark. "Unfortunately," he continued, "some evangelicals regard the Bible *only* as divine and not also a human product. Many seminary students start out thinking that way. I once looked over a student's shoulder while he was translating Greek in a workbook and said, 'That must be from the Gospel of Mark because the grammar is so bad.' The student was surprised. I said, "Well, yeah, he's one of the worst writers of Greek in the New Testament.' But that doesn't impact inspiration because we're dealing with what the product *is*, not how it's communicated. If Mark Twain can say 'ain't' and it's considered good writing, then you can have Mark do the same kind of thing."

"Now, finish this sentence," I said. "When Christians say the Bible is *inerrant*, they mean..."

"They mean a number of things," Wallace responded. "For some, it's almost a magic-wand approach, where the Bible is treated like a modern scientific and historical textbook that's letter-perfect. Some Christians would say, for example, that the words of Jesus are in red letters because that's *exactly* what he said.

"Well, if you compare the same incident in different Gospels, you'll notice some differences in wording. That's fine as long as we're not thinking in terms of quotations being nailed exactly, like a tape recorder. They didn't even have quotation marks in Greek. In ancient historiography, they were concerned with correctly getting the gist of what was said.

"The other view of inerrancy is to say the Bible is true in what it touches. So we can't treat it like a scientific book or a 21st-century historical document."

"How do you define *infallibility*?" I asked.

"My definition of *infallibility* is that the Bible is true in what it *teaches*. My definition of *inerrancy* is that the Bible is true in what it *touches*. So infallibility is a more foundational doctrine, which says the Bible is true with reference to faith and practice. Inerrancy is built on this doctrine, but it goes further, saying the Bible is also true when it comes to dealing with historical issues, but we still have to look at it in light of first-century historical practices."

THE PROTECTIVE SHELL

I've heard people say, "Find me one error, and I'll throw out the whole Bible." I wondered what Wallace thought about that. "What if you found an incontrovertible error in the Bible?" I asked. "How would you react?"

He thought for a moment, then replied. "It wouldn't affect my foundational view of Christ. I don't start by saying, 'If the Bible has a few mistakes, then I have to throw it all out.' That's not a logical position. We don't take that attitude toward any other ancient historical writings. For instance, did the first-century Jewish historian Josephus need to be inerrant before we could affirm that he got *anything* right?

"If we do that to the Bible, then we're putting it on a pedestal and just inviting people to try to knock it off. We've basically turned the Bible into the fourth person of the Trinity, as if it should be worshipped. What we need to do with Scripture instead is say that it's a great witness to the person of Jesus Christ and the acts of God in history. Now, is it more than that? Yes, I believe so. But whether it is or not, my salvation is still secure in Christ."

"So it's not necessary for a person to believe in inerrancy to be a Christian?" I asked.

"Personally, I believe in inerrancy," he began. "However, I wouldn't consider inerrancy to be a primary or essential doctrine for saving faith. It's what I call a 'protective shell' doctrine. Picture concentric circles with the essential doctrines of Christ and salvation at the core. A little bit further out are some other doctrines until, finally, outside of everything is inerrancy. Inerrancy is intended to protect these inner doctrines. But if inerrancy isn't true, does that mean that infallibility isn't true? No. It's a non sequitur to say I can't trust the Bible in the minutiae of history, so therefore I can't trust it in matters of faith and practice."

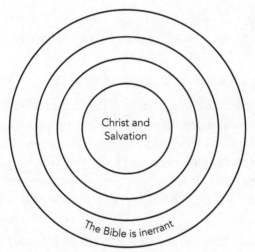

I nodded as he talked to indicate I was following his line of thinking. "With that concentric-circle approach, then, a supposed error in the New Testament shouldn't be fatal to a person's faith," I said.

"Absolutely," he replied without hesitation. "It might affect inerrancy, which is an outer-shell doctrine. But dismantling that wouldn't affect Christ, who's a core doctrine."

THE CORE OF THE GOSPELS

Wallace paused. "May I tell you a story about this?" he asked.

"Please," I said.

"Some years ago I met a Muslim girl who was interested in Christianity," he said. "She came to me with six handwritten, single-spaced pages of supposed discrepancies in the Gospels. She'd been taught by Muslims that if you can find one error in the Gospels, then you can't believe anything they say. She said to me, 'You're going to have to answer every single one of these before I can believe anything about Christianity.'

"My response was, 'Don't you think this list proves that the writers didn't conspire and collude when they wrote their Gospels?'

"She said, 'I've never thought of it that way.'

"I said, 'What you need to do is look at the places where the Gospels don't disagree at all. And what do you find? You find a core message that is revolutionary: Jesus was confessed as the Messiah by his disciples, he performed miracles and healed people, he forgave sins, he prophesied his own death and resurrection, he died on a Roman cross, and he was raised bodily from the dead.

"'So now, what are you going to do with Jesus? Even if the Gospel writers have differences in their accounts—whether we should really call them "discrepancies" is a topic for later—then this only adds to their credibility by showing they weren't huddled together in a corner cooking all of this up. Doesn't their agreement on an absolute core of central beliefs suggest that they got the basics right, precisely because they were reporting on the same events?'"

"What happened to her?" I asked.

"Two weeks later she became a Christian, and now she's a student at Dallas Seminary. My point is this: Inerrancy is important, but the gospel is bigger than inerrancy.

"As one British scholar said, 'We should treat the Bible like any other book in order to show it's not like any other book.' That's better than the opposite position that has become an evangelical mantra: 'Hands off the Bible—we don't want people to find any mistakes in it because we hold to inerrancy.'

"I'm not saying doctrines like inerrancy and infallibility aren't important," he went on. "I'm just saying they're not necessary for salvation. However, they are important for spiritual health and growth."

"How so?"

"If you doubt whether the Bible is an authoritative guide for faith and practice, it will inevitably affect your spiritual journey. You might begin questioning passages that are clear in their meaning, but they're too convicting for you, so you reject them. You begin to pick and choose out of the Bible what you want to believe and obey."

Wallace summed up his perspective. "Whatever you do with this," he urged, "don't throw out Christ if you're going to question inerrancy. Personally, I believe in inerrancy, but I'm not going to die for inerrancy. I will die for Christ. That's where my heart is because that's where salvation is," he said with conviction.

"The Bible wasn't hanged on the cross; Jesus was."

THE TELEPHONE GAME

Some people have compared the Bible to the children's game of telephone. You likely played this game as a child. A short message is communicated by whispering it in a person's ear. That person then whispers it into the next person's ear and so on until the message has been passed to everyone who's playing the game. The last person to get the message then says it out loud, and it's inevitable the message has become mixed up by this point.

The implication is that because the written Bible we have today was passed on through many generations, people simply can't trust what the New Testament says anymore. In short, we can't have any confidence today's Bible accurately represents the original text.

Wallace, however, said that analogy breaks down at several key points.

"First of all," he said, "rather than having one stream of transmission, we have multiple streams. If you think about that game of telephone, it might work like this: You have three lines of people all passing the same message, from the same source, down to one final recipient. By the time the last person gets all three messages, there would certainly be differences in those messages, but there would also be similarities. With a little detective work, you could figure out much of what the original message was by comparing the three different reports. Of course, you'd still have a lot of doubt as to whether you got it right.

"A second difference with the telephone game," he continued, "is that rather than dealing with an *oral* tradition, textual criticism deals with a *written* tradition. Now, if each person in the line wrote down what he heard from the person in front of him, the chances of garbling the message would be remote— and you'd have a pretty boring game!" he added with a smile.

"A third difference is that the textual critic—the person trying to reconstruct what the original message was—doesn't have to rely on that last person in the chain. He can talk to several people who are closer to the original source."

His conclusion? "Putting all this together, the cross-checks among the various streams of transmission, the examination of earlier copies—often exceedingly early—and the written records rather than oral tradition make textual criticism quite a bit more exacting and precise than the game of telephone."

THE TEXTUAL CRITIC GAME

There is, however, another game that does demonstrate the effectiveness of textual criticism. Wallace has conducted seminars for the past 30 years at universities and in other settings in which his goal is to give a practical demonstration of how textual criticism can succeed in reconstructing a missing text.

"In the game, numerous people serve as 'scribes' who copy out an ancient text on a Friday night," he said. "There are six generations of copies. The scribes all make mistakes, intentionally or unintentionally. In fact, the resultant copies are actually significantly more corrupt than the manuscript copies of the New Testament."

"How corrupt?" I asked.

"For a 50-word document, they're able to produce hundreds of textual variants," he said. "The next morning, the rest of the folks at the seminar get to work as textual critics, with the scribes as silent onlookers. But they don't have all the manuscripts to work with. The earliest copies were destroyed or lost. And there are many breaks in the chain. But the textual critics do the best they can with the materials they have.

"After about two hours of work, they come up with what

they think the original text said. There are some doubts at almost every turn. But remarkably, even with the doubts, the core idea is hardly changed. Sometimes the doubts have to do with *too* versus *also*, or *shall* versus *will*. Then I show the group the original text, and we compare the two texts, line by line, word by word."

"How successful are these amateur textual critics?" I asked.

"Altogether, I've conducted this seminar more than 50 times in churches, colleges, and seminaries—and we've never missed reconstructing the original text by more than three words. In fact, we were off by three words only once. Often, the group has gotten the original wording exactly right—and the essential message of the original is always intact. Sometimes people break out into spontaneous applause at the end!"

"What's the lesson, then?" I asked.

"It's basically this," he said. "If people who know nothing about textual criticism can reconstruct a text that has become terribly corrupted, then isn't it likely that those who are trained in textual criticism can do the same with the New Testament?"

QUANTITY AND QUALITY

As Wallace's seminar demonstrates, having a handful of copies can help even amateur sleuths determine the wording of the missing original text. Scholars trying to reconstruct the text of the New Testament, however, have thousands of manuscripts to work with. The more copies, the easier it is to discern the contents of the original. Given the centrality of New Testament documents to textual criticism, I asked Wallace to talk about their quantity and quality.

"Quite simply, we have more witnesses to the text of the New Testament than to any other ancient Greek or Latin literature," he declared.

"Exactly how many copies are in existence?" I asked.

"We have more than 5,700 Greek copies of the New Testament. When I started seminary, there were 4,800, but more and more have been discovered. There are another 10,000 copies in Latin. Then there are versions in other languages—Coptic, Syriac, Armenian, Georgian, and so on. These are estimated to number between 10,000 and 15,000. So right there we've got 25,000 to 30,000 handwritten copies of the New Testament."

"But aren't many of these merely fragments?" I asked.

"A great majority of these manuscripts are complete for the purposes that the scribes intended. For example, some manuscripts were intended just to include the Gospels; others, just Paul's letters. Only 60 Greek manuscripts have the entire New Testament, but that doesn't mean most manuscripts are fragmentary. Most are complete for the purposes intended," Wallace said.

"Now, if we were to destroy all of these manuscripts, would we be left without a New Testament?" he asked. Without waiting for my response, he said, "Not at all. The ancient church fathers quoted so often from the New Testament that it would be possible to reconstruct almost the entire New Testament from their writings alone. All told, there are more than one *million* quotations of the New Testament in their writings. They date as early as the first century and continue through the thirteenth century, so they're extremely valuable for determining the wording of the New Testament text.

"The quantity and quality of the New Testament manuscripts are unequalled in the ancient Greco-Roman world. The average ancient Greek author has fewer than 20 copies of his works still in existence, and even those appeared 500 to 1,000 years after they were written. If you stacked the works of other ancient writers on top of each other, they'd be about four feet tall. Stack up copies of the New Testament, and they'd reach more than a mile high—and, again, that doesn't include quotations from the church fathers."

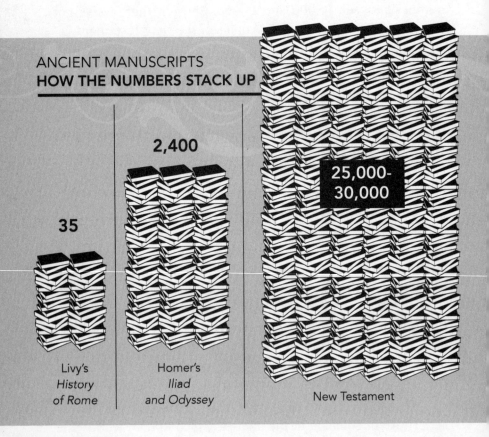

ANCIENT MANUSCRIPTS
HOW THE NUMBERS STACK UP

35

2,400

25,000-
30,000

Livy's
History
of Rome

Homer's
Iliad
and Odyssey

New Testament

DEALING WITH DIFFERENCES

Among the disclosures that alarmed Bart Ehrman's readers was one that said there are somewhere between 200,000 and 400,000 differences between New Testament manuscripts—in fact, more differences than the 138,162 words in the published Greek New Testament. This was old news to textual critics, but it was shocking to the general public. Yet are these differences really significant—and do they jeopardize the message of the Gospels and their depiction of Jesus?

"Tell me about these differences—how are they counted, and how did they come about?" I asked Wallace.

"If there's any manuscript or church father that has a different word in one place, then that counts as a 'textual variant,'" Wallace explained. "If you have a thousand manuscripts that have, for instance, 'Lord' in John 4:1 and all the rest of the manuscripts have 'Jesus,' then that still counts as only one variant. If a single 14th-century manuscript misspells a word, that counts as a variant."

"What are the most common variants?" I asked.

"Far and away, the most common are spelling variations, even when the misspelling in Greek makes absolutely no difference in the meaning of the word," he said.

"For example, the most common textual variant involves what's called a 'movable *nu*.' The Greek letter *nu*—or 'n'—is used at the end of a word when the next word starts with a vowel. It's like in English where you have an indefinite article—*an* apple or *a* book. It means the same thing. Whether or not a *nu* appears in these words has absolutely no effect on their meanings. Yet these are still recorded as textual variants.

"Another example is that every time you see the name *John*, it's either spelled with one or two n's. Textual critics have to record that as a textual variant, even though in English it still comes out as 'John' every time. It doesn't make any difference. The point is that it's not spelled *Mary*. Somewhere between 70 to 80 percent of all textual variants are spelling differences that can't even be translated into English and have zero impact on meaning."

I did some quick mental math: Taking the high estimate of 400,000 New Testament variants, that would mean 280,000 to 320,000 of them would be inconsequential differences in spelling. "Please, continue," I said to Wallace.

"Then you've got nonsense errors, where a scribe was inattentive and made a mistake that's an obvious no-brainer to spot," he said. "For example, in a manuscript in the Smithsonian Institution, one scribe wrote the word *and* when he meant to write *Lord*. The words look somewhat similar in Greek—*kai* versus *kurios*. But it was obvious that the word *and* doesn't fit the context. So in these cases, it's easy to reconstruct the right word.

"There are also variants involving synonyms. Does a particular passage say, 'When Jesus knew' or 'When the Lord knew'? We're not sure which one goes back to the original, but both words are true. A lot of variants involve the Greek practice of using a definite article with a proper name, which we don't do in English. For example, a manuscript might refer to 'the Mary' or 'the Joseph,' but the scribe might have simply written 'Mary' or 'Joseph.' Again, there's no impact on meaning, but they're all counted as variants.

"On top of that, you've got variants that can't even be translated into English. Greek is a highly inflected language. That means the order of words in Greek isn't as important as it is in English. For example, there are 16 different ways in Greek to say, 'Jesus loves Paul,' and they would be translated into English the very same way. Still, if there's a difference in the order of words, even if the meaning is unaffected, it counts as a textual variant."

Wallace stopped for a moment to consider the situation. "So if we have approximately 200,000 to 400,000 variants among the Greek manuscripts, well, I'm just shocked there are so few!" he declared. "What would the potential number be? Tens of *millions*! Part of the reason we have so many variants is because we have so many manuscripts. And we're glad we have so many manuscripts—it helps us immensely in getting back to the original."

TEXTUAL DIFFERENCES IN NEW TESTAMENT MANUSCRIPTS

Total Variants: Up to 400,000

Different Synonyms or Sentence Structure, etc.: Around 76,000

Variants That Affect the Meaning to Some Degree and Have a Decent Chance of Going Back to the Original: Around 4,000 (or 1 percent of total)

Variations in Spelling: Up to 320,000

I asked, "How many textual variants really make a difference?"

"Only about 1 percent of variants are both meaningful—which means they affect the meaning of the text to some degree—and viable, which means they have a decent chance of going back to the original text."

"Still, that's a pretty big number," I said.

"But most of these are not very significant at all," he said.

"Give me an example."

"Okay," he replied. "I'll describe two of the most notorious issues. One involves Romans 5:1. Did Paul say, 'We *have* peace' or '*Let us have* peace'? The difference amounts to one letter in the Greek. Scholars are split on this, but the big point is that neither variant is a contradiction of the teachings of Scripture.

"Another famous example is 1 John 1:4. The verse says either, 'Thus we are writing these things so that *our* joy may be complete,' or 'Thus we are writing these things so that *your* joy may be complete.' There's ancient testimony for both readings. So, yes, the meaning is affected, but no foundational beliefs are in jeopardy. Either way, the obvious meaning of the verse is that the writing of this letter brings joy."

It was simply amazing to me that two of the most notorious textual issues are, in essence, so trivial in their implications.

INTENTIONAL CHANGES

There are a lot of reasons textual errors occur, many of them involving scribes who aren't paying enough attention. Ehrman puts a lot of emphasis, however, on scribes who intentionally altered the text as they reproduced it for the next generation of manuscripts.

"That idea makes people very nervous," I said to Wallace.

"Well, he's absolutely correct," Wallace replied. "Sometimes scribes did intentionally change the text."

"What's the most common reason?" I asked.

"They wanted to make the text clearer. Through the centuries, for example, the church started using sections of Scripture for daily readings. These are called 'lectionaries.' About 2,200 of our Greek manuscripts are lectionaries, which set out a year's worth of daily or weekly Scripture readings.

"Here's what happened: In the Gospel of Mark, there are 89 verses in a row where the name of Jesus isn't mentioned once. Just pronouns are used, with 'he' referring to Jesus. Well, if you excerpt a passage for a daily lectionary reading, you can't start with: 'When he was going someplace...' The reader wouldn't know to whom you were referring. So it was logical for the scribe to replace 'he' with 'Jesus' in order to be more specific in the lectionary. But it's counted as a variant every single time."

I interrupted. "Ehrman says: 'It would be wrong...to say— as people sometimes do—that the changes in our text have no real bearing on what the texts mean or on the theological conclusion that one draws from them.... Just the opposite is the case.'[28] Exactly how many Christian doctrines are jeopardized by textual variants in the New Testament?"

"Let me repeat the basic thesis that has been argued since 1707," Wallace said. "No cardinal or essential doctrine is altered by any textual variant that has plausibility of going back to the original. The evidence for that has not changed to this day."

"What comes the closest?"

"Mark 9:29 could impact ortho*praxy*, which is right practice, but not ortho*doxy*, which is right belief. Here Jesus says you can't cast out a certain kind of demon except by prayer—and some manuscripts add, 'and fasting.' So if 'and fasting' is part of what Jesus said, then here's a textual variant that affects orthopraxy—is it necessary to fast in order to do certain kinds of exorcisms? But seriously, does my salvation depend on that? Most Christians have never even heard of that verse nor will they ever perform an exorcism."

"Back to your original point then."

"My original point is this: No cardinal doctrines are affected by any viable variants."

A FAVORITE STORY—AND A FRAUD?

It's one of the most beloved stories in the Bible: A woman caught in the act of adultery is brought before Jesus. It's really a trap—the Pharisees knew she should be stoned to death under the Law of Moses, and they wanted to test Jesus to see what he'd do.

Jesus bent down and began using his finger to write something in the dirt. Those words aren't recorded, promoting all sorts of speculation throughout the centuries. Finally, Jesus uttered these often-quoted words: "Let any one of you who is without sin be the first to throw a stone at her." Chastened, the Pharisees walked away one at a time, the oldest ones first. Once they were gone, Jesus said to the adulteress: "Woman, where are they? Has no one condemned you?" She replied, "No one, sir." Then Jesus said: "Then neither do I condemn you. Go now and leave your life of sin."[29]

The only problem with this story is that scholars have known for more than a century that it's not authentic. This was disturbing news to readers of Ehrman's book. Many people seemed to take the loss personally—and they began asking what else in their Bibles couldn't be trusted.

"This is one of those stories," Wallace said when I asked him about the adultery account, "that when you read it, you say, 'That takes my breath away! I'm just amazed at the love and the grace and the mercy of Jesus and how he could stand up to these Pharisees.' We say, 'I *want* this to be in the Bible.' And that's exactly what the copyists said. They read this as an independent story and ended up putting it in at least half a dozen different locations in John and Luke. It's as if the scribes said, 'I want this to go into my Bible, so I'm going to insert it here or here or here.'"

"So this was a story that came down through time?" I asked.

"Apparently, there were two different stories circulating about a woman who'd been caught in some sin and Jesus was merciful to her. More than likely, that much of the story was historically true, but it didn't end up in the Scriptures."

"But it's clear that the story in the Bible is not authentic," I said.

"There's a distinction we need to make," he replied. "Is it *literarily* authentic—in other words, did John actually write this story? My answer is an unquestionable no. Is it *historically* authentic? Did it really happen? My answer is a highly qualified yes—something may have happened with Jesus being merciful to a sinner, but the story was originally in a truncated form."

"Why have Bibles continued to include it?" I asked. "Doesn't that simply confuse readers?"

"Read any Bible translation, and you'll find a marginal note that says this [story] isn't found in the oldest manuscripts,"

Wallace said. "But people often don't read those. When Ehrman reports in the popular sphere that the story isn't authentic, people think they've been hoodwinked."

I picked up my New International Version of the Bible and flipped to the Gospel of John. Sure enough, there are rules at the top and bottom of the story in order to delineate it, as well as a note in the center of the page that says: "The earliest manuscripts and many other ancient witnesses do not have John 7:53–8:11." But how many people, I wondered, really understand the implications of that note?

"Are Bible publishers misleading people by putting it in?" I asked.

"I would be cautious about saying that," Wallace replied, "but they certainly could do a better job of saying, 'This is not found in the oldest manuscripts, and furthermore the editors of this translation do not believe these words are authentic.' Otherwise you're setting people up for disillusionment if they get this information elsewhere. It's a Chicken Little mentality that says, 'Oh no, I never knew that these precious 12 verses aren't authentic—and what else are you not telling me?' But the fact is publishers *have* told them about it, and it's an exceptional circumstance. There's only one other passage that's even close to that length."

That's the topic I wanted to address next.

WHAT HAPPENED ON EASTER?

In November 2006, a 48-year-old woman died four hours after she was bitten by a timber rattlesnake during Sunday services in a Kentucky church. She was the seventh such fatality in Kentucky since 1980. In fact, after she died state legislators felt compelled to pass a law making it a misdemeanor to handle reptiles as part of religious services.[30]

The journalists reporting on the woman's death all said that according to the Gospel of Mark, believers in Jesus will be able to handle snakes without harm. None of them, however, noted that this verse—and, in fact, the last 12 verses of Mark—were not part of the original Gospel, but were added at a later date and aren't considered authentic.

This means the book of Mark ends with three women discovering the empty tomb of Jesus and being told by "a young man dressed in a white robe" that Jesus had risen from the dead. "They said nothing to anyone," concludes the Gospel, "because they were afraid" (Mark 16:8). The final 12 verses describe three post-crucifixion appearances by Jesus and say Christians will be able to pick up snakes without injury, as well as cast out demons, speak in new tongues, and heal the sick.

"Where do you think this ending came from?" I asked Wallace.

"I think Mark was writing about the distinctively unique individual who has ever lived, and he wanted to format the ending of his Gospel in a unique way, in which he leaves it open ended. He's essentially saying to readers, 'So what are *you* going to do with Jesus?'"

"Eliminating those 12 verses, then, really has no impact on the doctrine of the resurrection?"

"Not in the slightest. There's still a resurrection in Mark. It's prophesied, the angel attests to it, and the tomb is empty. But you can see why an early scribe would say, 'Oh no, we don't have a resurrection appearance, and this ends with the women being afraid.' I think a scribe in the second century essentially drew on the book of Acts, in which Paul gets bitten by a snake and people are speaking in tongues. He wanted to round out Mark's Gospel, so he put on that new ending."

"Why does the Bible still have it?"

"Once it's in the Bible, it's really hard to dislodge it. All Bibles have a note indicating this longer ending isn't in the oldest manuscripts. Some put these verses in smaller type or otherwise bracket it. Of the disputed verses in the Bible, this and the woman caught in adultery are by far the longest passages—and again, they're old news."

There is a third significant passage, however, and I wanted to ask Wallace about it.

IS THE TRINITY IN THE BIBLE?

Ehrman said, "The only passage in the entire Bible that explicitly delineates the doctrine of the Trinity" is found in 1 John 5:7-8 in the King James Version, which says: "For there are three that bear record in heaven, the Father, the Word, and the Holy Ghost: and these three are one."

"Wouldn't you agree that this is inauthentic?" I asked Wallace.

"Absolutely."

"Where did it come from?"

"That actually came from a homily in the eighth century. It was added to a Latin text and wasn't even translated into Greek until 1520. To date, we've found a grand total of four manuscripts that have it, all from the sixteenth or seventeenth centuries, plus four others that have it as a marginal note in a later hand. It's obviously inauthentic."

I said, "I got a note from a woman recently who wrote, 'I've got a great verse for you to support the Trinity. And, by the way, you only find it in the King James Version. Take a look; it's there!' So some people still think it's authentic."

Wallace sighed. "We need to do a better job of training the church. The fact that we've been dumbing down the church for so long is just a crime, and now people are panicking when they hear about this sort of thing. You don't even find this in other translations, except perhaps in a footnote."

"Atheist Frank Zindler says that deleting this inauthentic reference 'leaves Christians without biblical proof of the Trinity,'" I observed.[31]

Wallace reacted firmly. "I'm going to be uncharitable here: That's just such a stupid comment, I can hardly believe it," he said. "Christians as far back as the Council of Constantinople in AD 381 and Chalcedon in AD 451 made explicit statements affirming the Trinity—obviously, they didn't need this later, inauthentic passage to see it.

"The Bible clearly contains these four truths: The Father is God, Jesus is God, the Holy Spirit is God, and there's only one God," Wallace declared. "And that's the Trinity."

THE HOLY GRAIL

Wallace had brought balance and perspective to the issue of whether the New Testament's text can be trusted. In the end, there's no dispute over the fundamentals. As for Jesus, there's nothing that would compel a new perspective on his life, character, miracles, resurrection, or divinity.

I glanced at my watch; it was getting late. I had one more issue I wanted to raise, but I didn't relish asking Wallace about it. This wasn't a critique by a reputable scholar, but claims made by the authors of *Holy Blood, Holy Grail*—a book that's been discredited by historians in so many ways. Still, I believe its widespread popularity made it worth addressing.

"The authors of *Holy Blood, Holy Grail* claim that in AD 303, Emperor Diocletian destroyed all Christian writings that could be found," I said. "Later, Emperor Constantine commissioned new versions. These three authors claim that these were the writings that gave Jesus his unique status as the Son of God."[32]

Wallace looked exasperated. "Good grief!" he exclaimed. "That's just loony! Do these authors know *anything* about history at all? Diocletian did not destroy all the Christian manuscripts. He did destroy several, but we have more than four dozen in Greek alone from before the time Diocletian was supposed to have destroyed them all. And these manuscripts have numerous passages—John 1:1; John 1:18; John 20:28; Titus 2:13; Hebrews 1:8; 2 Peter 1:1—that affirm the deity of Jesus. So it's nonsense to say Jesus' deity wasn't invented until the fourth century, when you've already got the evidence in earlier manuscripts.

"Besides, we still have lots and lots of quotations by church fathers prior to the fourth century. In about AD 110, Ignatius calls Jesus 'our God' and then says, 'the blood of God,' referring to Jesus. Where does he get this idea if it wasn't invented until more than 200 years later? You can't make that kind of a claim and be any kind of a responsible historian. No historian would ever even entertain that kind of stupidity."

"Yet apparently millions of people believe it," I said. "What does that do to you as a scholar?"

"First, we have to quit marginalizing Scripture," he said. "We can't treat the Bible with kid gloves. We really need to wrestle with the issues because our faith depends on it. And second, we need to quit turning Jesus into our buddy. He's the sovereign Lord of the universe, and we need to understand that and respond accordingly."

"Do you believe God has accurately preserved enough for us to know him and his truth?"

"Absolutely. Do we have all the essentials? Yes. Do we have all the particulars? No. But that's the task of a textual critic: To try to get back to the original. I'll spend the rest of my life looking at manuscripts—transcribing them, photographing them, and publishing them. We still won't recover the original wording in every single place. But I hope that by the end of my life we'll be a little bit closer—and that's a worthy goal."

WELL-PLACED TRUST

My interview with Wallace provided strong affirmation that my confidence in the New Testament text was abundantly warranted. None of the criticisms came even close to changing the biblical portrait of the real Jesus in any meaningful way.

As I drove away from Wallace's house that night, my mind flashed back to my interview several years earlier with Bruce M. Metzger, a scholar who was universally acknowledged as the greatest textual critic of his generation. In fact, Metzger was Ehrman's mentor at Princeton, and Ehrman even dedicated *Misquoting Jesus* to him, calling him "Doctor-Father" and saying he "taught me the field and continues to inspire me in my work."[33]

At the time we chatted, Metzger was 83 years old. Thinking back on it now, what fascinated me was how much his remarks from that day reflected what Wallace had just told me so many years later.

For instance, I remember asking Metzger, "So the variations [between manuscripts], when they occur, tend to be minor rather than substantive?"

"Yes, yes, that's correct," Metzger replied, adding, "the more significant variations do not overthrow any doctrine of the church."

Then I recall asking him how the many decades he'd spent intensely studying the New Testament's text had affected his personal faith.

"Oh," he said, sounding happy to discuss the topic, "it has increased the basis of my personal faith to see the firmness with which these materials have come down to us, with a multiplicity of copies, some of which are very ancient."

"So," I started to say, "scholarship has not diluted your faith—"

He jumped in before I could finish my sentence. "On the contrary," he stressed, "it has built it. I've asked questions all my life, I've dug into the text, I've studied this thoroughly, and today I know with confidence that my trust in Jesus has been well placed." He paused while his eyes surveyed my face. Then he added, for emphasis, "*Very* well placed."[34]

New Explanations Have Disproved Jesus' Resurrection

O utside a Chicago hospital on a humid summer night, a gunshot victim was unloaded from an ambulance and wheeled on a gurney into the emergency room. The teenager gestured toward his abdomen as he was rolled past reporters. "It doesn't even hurt!" he said with a nervous laugh, as if everyone there was his old friend. "It doesn't even hurt!"

A few hours later, he was dead.

A reporter on the streets of Chicago soon develops more than a passing acquaintance with death. Often, the people directly embroiled in an unfolding tragedy—the apartment fire, the car accident, the gang fight, the convenience store robbery gone awry—are too bewildered and disoriented to fully comprehend their predicament. But from the detached perspective of the reporter, the grim outcome is much more foreseeable. And when death finally does seize its victims, when their eyes stare blankly, then all hope is gone. They've spoken their last word, they've breathed their last breath, and their time is done—they won't be coming back.

That's why all this talk of Jesus' resurrection seemed so strange to me. It's staggering how quickly the body of a deceased person is reduced to a mere shell. The idea that a body could somehow become reanimated, especially after three days, could never quite get past my journalistic skepticism when I was an atheist.

As I documented in *The Case for Christ*, it was my investigation of the historical evidence that eventually convinced me the resurrection of Jesus really happened.[35] Since then, however, the resurrection has been subjected to new and more contentious attacks. Do any of these updated objections manage to crack this central pillar of Christianity?

At the forefront of the most recent challenges to the resurrection have been Muslims who clearly understand that discrediting the resurrection means nothing less than disproving the truth of Christianity. Muslims interpret the Qur'an as saying that Jesus never actually died on the cross, much less returned from the dead.[36]

Muslims aren't the only ones. A prominent Hindu leader declared in a 2007 speech that Jesus never died on the cross. "He was only injured and after treatment returned to India where he actually died," insisted K. S. Sudarshan, leader of a nationalist Hindu organization in India.[37]

Atheists, meanwhile, have been mounting ever-more-intense critiques of the resurrection. Much of it comes from scrappy skeptics on the Internet, many of whom lack scholarly credentials but certainly are passionate in their denunciations of the resurrection, spinning elaborate scenarios to try to explain it away. In 2005, Prometheus Books published an ambitious 545-page anthology called *The Empty Tomb* in which such skeptics as Michael Martin and Richard Carrier set out their alternative explanations for the Easter event. The Jesus Seminar's Robert M. Price is emphatic in the introduction: "Jesus," he declared, "is dead."[38]

I picked up the telephone to call one of the emerging authorities on the resurrection of Jesus, whose provocative books include an imaginary debate on the issues between the apostle Paul and the prophet Muhammad. I invited him over to my house for a chat. Once and for all, I was determined to get to the truth about the most current challenges to this cornerstone doctrine.

INTERVIEW #3: MICHAEL LICONA, MA, PHD (CAND.)

Six-foot-three and lanky, Michael Licona was once a second-degree black belt and award-winning instructor in *tae kwon do*, a modern Korean martial art that is a lethal form of one-on-one combat. While a ruptured disk has sidelined his fighting in the ring, Licona has morphed into a respected and accomplished participant in another kind of contest, this time involving intellectual clashes over the historical claims of Christianity.

Licona's faith was sharpened by a period of doubt that he went through at the end of his graduate studies in 1985. His questions about whether Christianity was true nearly led him to abandon the beliefs he'd held since the age of 10. Instead, his renewed investigation of the evidence for Christianity and a number of other major world religions, as well as his in-depth study of atheism, solidified his conviction that Christianity rests on a firm historical foundation.

THE HISTORIAN AND THE RESURRECTION

I didn't waste any time before launching into my initial line of questions about how historians can investigate an ancient—and supposedly supernatural—event like Jesus returning from the dead.

"Isn't it true that a miracle like the resurrection is actually outside the purview of historians to investigate?" I asked. "If a historian allows for the possibility of the miraculous, then doesn't that throw history up for grabs? You could invoke a miraculous explanation for all kinds of things that happened in the past."

"No, because you have to apply historical criteria to determine the best explanation for what occurred," Licona said.

He quickly thought of an illustration. "For example, *Aesop's Fables* describes animals talking in ancient Greece. Well, did they talk or didn't they?"

I wasn't sure where he was going with this. "Okay," I said, "how would you assess that?"

"Well, when we examine the genre of *Aesop's Fables*, we find that these stories were not meant to be interpreted literally. Besides, there are no credible eyewitness accounts and there's no corroboration from other sources. So the historian would say there's no good evidence that *Aesop's Fables* reports actual historical events," he replied.

"But regarding Jesus' resurrection, we find that the Gospels fit into the genre of ancient biographies. We know that ancient biographies were intended to be regarded as history to varying degrees. We've got early accounts that can't be explained away by legendary development, we've got multiple independent sources, we've got eyewitnesses, and we've got a degree of corroboration from outsiders. We've also got enemy attestation; that is, affirmation from people like Saul of Tarsus, who was a critic of Christianity until he saw the evidence for himself that Jesus had returned from the dead. So weighing the historical criteria, there's no reason to believe the stories in *Aesop's Fables* are true, but there are good reasons to believe the resurrection happened."

THE HISTORIAN'S THREE RS

I was fascinated by the approach historians take in evaluating the evidence that Jesus returned from the dead. "How would a historian begin investigating something like the resurrection?" I asked.

Licona put down his water glass, unbuttoned the cuffs of his shirt, and rolled up his sleeves as if he were getting ready for a lengthy discussion. "You've heard of the three Rs of an elementary education: Reading, 'Riting, and 'Rithmetic? Well, there are also three Rs for doing good history: Relevant Sources, Responsible Method, and Restrained Results."

1. RELEVANT SOURCES

He went on to explain what he meant. "First," he said, "historians must identify all the relevant sources."

"All right," I said. "What would those be in the case of Jesus?"

"There are the New Testament writings; a few secular sources who mention Jesus, such as Josephus, Tacitus, and Pliny the Younger; the apologists, who were early defenders of Christianity; and even the Gnostic writings. We also want to examine the next generation after the apostles."

2. RESPONSIBLE METHOD

"Once all the relevant sources have been identified," he continued, "we have to apply responsible method. This means assigning the greatest weight to reports that are early, eyewitness, enemy, embarrassing, and corroborated by others."

"And what do you mean by 'restrained results'?" I wondered out loud.

3. RESTRAINED RESULTS

"This means historians shouldn't claim more than the evidence warrants. This is where such scholars as John Dominic Crossan and Elaine Pagels get on thin ice. Their imaginations are very good—and I mean that in a positive sense—but I believe their methods are sometimes questionable and their results unrestrained. In the end they're embarrassed because their views are founded upon an early dating for the Gospel of Thomas, and in Crossan's case, the Secret Gospel of Mark. Now it appears that Thomas may very well have been written after AD 170 and that the Secret Gospel of Mark wasn't actually composed until the twentieth century! What does that say about their revisionist theories, which rely on a much earlier dating of these sources?"

THE MINIMAL FACTS APPROACH

Licona's point was well taken, especially in light of my earlier interview with Craig Evans about "alternative gospels." At the same time, I knew that Licona, like all scholars, also brings his own prejudices to the discussion.

"What about biases?" I said. "You can't deny that you see the historical evidence through the lens of your own prejudices."

"No, I can't. Nobody is exempt, including theists, deists, atheists, or whatever—we all have our biases, and there's no way to overcome them," Licona said. He gestured toward me. "Lee, you're trained as a journalist. You know you can try to minimize your biases, but you can't eliminate them. That's why you have to put certain checks and balances in place. This is what historian Gary Habermas did in creating what's called the 'minimal facts approach' to the resurrection, which he and I wrote about in our book *The Case for the Resurrection of Jesus*."

"How does this help keep biases in check?"

"Under this approach, we only consider facts that meet two criteria. First, there must be very strong historical evidence supporting them. And second, the evidence must be so strong that the vast majority of today's scholars on the subject—including skeptical ones—accept these as historical facts. You're never going to get everyone to agree. There are always people who deny the Holocaust or question whether Jesus ever existed, but they're on the fringe."

"History isn't a vote," I interjected. "Are you saying people should accept these facts just because a lot of scholars do?"

"No, we're saying that this evidence is so good that even skeptical scholars are convinced by it. Your bias could be leading you to a conclusion, but if the evidence is also leading someone with vastly different beliefs toward the same conclusion, then there's a good chance the conclusion is true. This serves as a check on bias. It's not foolproof, but it's very helpful."

With that background in place, I issued Licona a challenge. "Use only the minimal facts," I said, "and let's see how strong a case you can build for Jesus rising from the dead."

Licona smiled and moved to the edge of the couch. "I thought you'd never ask," he said with a chuckle. "I'll use just five minimal facts—and you can decide for yourself how persuasive the case is."

FACT #1: JESUS WAS KILLED BY CRUCIFIXION

"The first fact is Jesus' crucifixion," he began. "Even an extreme liberal like Crossan says: 'That he was crucified is as sure as anything historical ever can be.'[39] Skeptic James Tabor says, 'I think we need have no doubt that given Jesus' execution by Roman crucifixion he was truly *dead*.'[40] Both Gerd Lüdemann, who's an atheistic New Testament critic, and Bart Ehrman, who's an agnostic, call the crucifixion an indisputable fact. Why? First of all, because all four Gospels report it."

I put up my hand. "Whoa! Hold on!" I insisted. "Are you operating under the assumption that the Bible is the inspired word of God?"

Licona seemed glad I had brought up the issue. "Let me clarify something: For the purposes of examining the evidence, I'm not considering the Bible to be inerrant, inspired, or Scripture of any kind," he replied. "I'm simply accepting it for what it unquestionably is—a set of ancient documents that can be subjected to historical scrutiny like any other accounts from antiquity. In other words, regardless of my personal beliefs, I'm not giving the Bible a privileged position in my investigation. I'm applying the same historical standards to it that I would apply to any other ancient document."

With that caveat, he went on with his case. "Now, beyond the four Gospels, we also have a number of non-Christian sources that corroborate the crucifixion. For instance, the historian Tacitus said Jesus 'suffered the extreme penalty during the reign of Tiberius.'[41] The Jewish historian Josephus reports that Pilate 'condemned him to be crucified.'[42] Lucian of Samosata, who was a Greek satirist, mentions the crucifixion, and Mara Bar-Serapion, who was a pagan, confirms Jesus was executed."

"What were the odds of surviving crucifixion?"

"Extremely small. You saw *The Passion of the Christ*, right? Even though not all of the film was historically accurate, it did depict the extreme brutality of Roman scourging and crucifixion. Witnesses in the ancient world reported victims being whipped so severely that their intestines and veins were laid bare."

"Did anyone ever survive it?"

"Interestingly, Josephus does mention three friends who were crucified during the fall of Jerusalem. He doesn't say how long they'd been on the cross, but he intervened with the Roman commander Titus, who ordered all three removed immediately and provided the best medical attention Rome had to offer. Still, two of them died. So even under the best of conditions, a victim was unlikely to survive crucifixion. And there is no evidence at all that Jesus was removed prematurely or that he was provided any medical attention whatsoever, much less Rome's best."

"We're dealing with a pretty primitive culture," I observed. "Were they competent enough to be sure that Jesus was dead?"

"I'm confident they were. You've got Roman soldiers carrying out executions all the time. It was their job. They were good at it. Besides, death by crucifixion was basically a slow and agonizing demise by asphyxiation because of the difficulty in breathing created by the victim's position on the cross. And that's something you can't fake.

"Lee, this first fact is as solid as anything in ancient history: Jesus was crucified and died as a result. The scholarly consensus—again, even among those who are skeptical toward the resurrection—is absolutely overwhelming. To deny it would be to take a marginal position that would get you laughed out of the academic world."

With that firmly established, Licona advanced to his next minimal fact.

FACT #2: JESUS' DISCIPLES BELIEVED HE ROSE AND APPEARED TO THEM

"The second fact is the disciples' beliefs that Jesus actually returned from the dead and appeared to them," Licona said. "There are three strands of evidence for this: Paul's testimony about the disciples, oral traditions that passed through the early church, and the written works of the early church.

"Paul is important because he reports knowing some of the disciples personally, including Peter, James, and John. Acts confirms this.[43] Paul knew the apostles and reports that they claimed—just as he did—that Jesus had returned from the dead.

"Then we have oral tradition. Obviously, people in those days didn't have tape recorders, and few people could read, so they relied on verbal transmission for passing along what happened until it was later written down. Scholars have identified several places in which this oral tradition has been copied into the New Testament in the form of creeds, hymns, and sermon summaries. This is really significant because the oral tradition must have existed before the New Testament writings in order for the New Testament authors to have included them."

"So it's early."

"Very early, which weighs heavily in their favor, as any historian will tell you. For example, we have creeds that laid out basic doctrines in a form that was easily memorized. One of the earliest and most important creeds was relayed by Paul in his first letter to the Corinthian church, which was written about AD 55. It says:

For what I received I passed on to you as of first importance: that Christ died for our sins according to the Scriptures, that he was buried, that he was raised on the third day according to the Scriptures, and that he appeared to Peter, and then to the Twelve. After that, he appeared to more than five hundred of the brothers at the same time, most of whom are still living, though some have fallen asleep. Then he appeared to James, then to all the apostles.[44]

"Many scholars believe Paul received this creed from Peter and James while he was visiting with them in Jerusalem three years after his conversion. That would be within five years of the crucifixion."

Licona's eyes got wide. "Think about that—it's really amazing!" he declared, his voice rising in genuine astonishment. "As one expert said, 'This is the sort of data that historians of antiquity drool over.'[45] Not only is it extremely early, but it was apparently given to Paul by eyewitnesses or others he deemed reliable, which heightens its credibility even more.

"And we've got even more oral tradition—for instance, the New Testament preserves several summaries of the preaching of the apostles, and they're not at all ambiguous: They declare that Jesus rose bodily from the dead.

"Finally, we have written sources, such as Matthew, Mark, Luke, and John. It's widely accepted, even among skeptical historians, that the Gospels were written in the first century. Even very liberal scholars will concede that we have four biographies written within 70 years of Jesus' life that unambiguously report the disciples' claims that Jesus rose from the dead.

"Then we have the writings of the generation after the apostles, people who were said to have known the apostles or were close to others who did. There's a strong likelihood that their writings reflect the teachings of the apostles themselves. And what do they say? That the apostles were dramatically impacted by Jesus' resurrection.

"Consider Polycarp, for example. The writer Irenaeus reports that Polycarp was 'instructed by apostles, and conversed with many who had seen Christ,' including John; that he 'recalled their very words'; and that he 'always taught the things which he had learned from the apostles.'[46] Tertullian confirms that John appointed Polycarp as bishop of the church in Smyrna.

"Around AD 110, Polycarp wrote a letter to the Philippian church in which he mentions the resurrection of Jesus no fewer than five times. He was referring to Paul and the other apostles when he said: 'For they did not love the present age, but him who died for our benefit and for our sake was raised by God.'[47]

"So think about the depth of evidence we have in these three categories: Paul, oral tradition, and written reports. In all, we've got nine sources that reflect multiple, very early, and eyewitness testimonies to the disciples' claims that they had seen the risen Jesus. This is something the disciples believed to the core of their beings."

"How do you know that?"

"Because we have evidence that the disciples had been transformed to the point where they were willing to endure persecution and even martyrdom. We find this in multiple accounts inside and outside the New Testament.

"Just read through Acts and you'll see how the disciples were willing to suffer for their conviction that Jesus rose from the dead. The church fathers Clement, Polycarp, Ignatius, Tertullian, and Origen—they all confirm this. In fact, we've got at least seven early sources testifying that the disciples willingly suffered in defense of their beliefs—and if we include the martyrdoms of Paul and Jesus' half-brother James, we have 11 sources."

"But," I objected, "people of other faiths have been willing to die for their beliefs through the ages—so what does the martyrdom of the disciples really prove?"

"First, it means that they certainly regarded their beliefs to be true," he said. "They didn't willfully lie about this. Liars make poor martyrs. Second, the disciples didn't just *believe* Jesus rose from the dead, but they knew for a fact whether he did. They were on the scene and able to ascertain for sure that he'd been resurrected. So it was for the *truth* of the resurrection that they were willing to die.

"This is totally different from a modern-day Islamic terrorist or others who are willing to die for their beliefs. These people can only have faith that their beliefs are true, but they aren't in a position to know for sure. The disciples, on the other hand, knew for a *fact* whether the resurrection had truly occurred— and knowing the *truth*, they were willing to die for the belief that they had.

"Even the atheist Gerd Lüdemann conceded: 'It may be taken as historically certain that Peter and the disciples had experiences after Jesus' death in which Jesus appeared to them as the risen Christ.'[48] Now, he claims this was the result of visions, which I simply don't believe is a credible explanation. But he's conceding that their experiences actually occurred."

The case for the disciples encountering what they believed to be the risen Jesus did, indeed, seem strong. Still, skeptics have raised some fresh objections in recent years. Rather than sidetrack Licona at this point, however, I decided to wait until he finished describing his five minimal facts. At that point, I could examine him in more depth.

"Go ahead," I said. "What's your third minimal fact?"

FACT #3: THE CONVERSION OF THE CHURCH PERSECUTOR PAUL

"We know from multiple sources that Paul—who was then known as Saul of Tarsus—was an enemy of the church and committed to persecuting the faithful," Licona continued. "But Paul himself says he was converted to a follower of Jesus because he personally encountered the resurrected Jesus.[49] So we have Jesus' resurrection attested by friend and foe alike, which is very significant.

"Then we have six ancient sources in addition to Paul—such as Luke, Clement of Rome, Polycarp, Tertullian, Dionysius of Corinth, and Origen—reporting that Paul was willing to suffer continuously and even die for his beliefs. Again, liars make poor martyrs. So we can be confident that Paul not only claimed the risen Jesus appeared to him, but that he really believed it.

"Saul was a most unlikely candidate for conversion. His mindset was to oppose the Christian movement that he believed was following a false Messiah. His radical transformation from persecutor to missionary demands an explanation—and I think the best explanation is that he's telling the truth when he says he met the risen Jesus on the road to Damascus.

"He had nothing to gain in this world—except his own suffering and martyrdom—for making this up."

FACT #4: THE CONVERSION OF THE SKEPTIC JAMES, JESUS' HALF-BROTHER

"The next minimal fact involves James, the half-brother of Jesus," Licona said.

"Some people might be surprised that Jesus had siblings," I commented.

"Well, the Gospels tell us that Jesus had at least four half-brothers—James, Joseph, Judas, and Simon—as well as half-sisters whose names we don't know.[50] We also have good evidence that James was not a follower of Jesus during Jesus' lifetime."

"How do you know?"

"Mark and John both report that none of Jesus' brothers believed in him.[51] In fact, John's passage is particularly interesting. It suggests that Jesus' brothers had heard about his alleged miracles but didn't believe the reports and were, in a sense, daring their brother to perform them in front of crowds. They were sort of taunting him!"[52]

"Do you have any other evidence for their skepticism?"

"At the crucifixion, to whom does Jesus entrust the care of his mother? Not to one of his half-brothers, who would be the natural choice, but to John, who was a believer. Why on earth would he do that? I think the inference is very strong: If James or any of his brothers had been believers, then they would have gotten the nod instead. So it's reasonable to conclude that none of them were believers, and Jesus was more concerned with his mother being entrusted into the hands of a spiritual brother.

"Then, however, the pivotal moment occurs: 1 Corinthians 15:7 tells us that the risen Jesus appeared to James. Again, this is an extremely early account that has all the earmarks of reliability. In fact, James may have been involved in passing along this creed to Paul, in which case James would be personally endorsing what the creed reports about him.

"As a result of his encounter with the risen Jesus, James doesn't just become a Christian, but he later becomes leader of the Jerusalem church. We know this from Acts and Galatians.[53] Actually, the resurrection so thoroughly convinced James that Jesus was the Messiah, James died as a martyr, as both Christian and non-Christian sources attest.[54]

"So here we have another example of a skeptic who was converted because of a personal encounter with the resurrected Lord and was willing to die for his convictions. In fact, critical scholar Reginald Fuller said that even if we didn't have the 1 Corinthians 15 account, 'we should have to invent' such a resurrection appearance to account for James' conversion and his elevation to the pastorate of the Jerusalem church, which was the center of ancient Christianity."[55]

Licona paused as if he'd finished his point. But something had occurred to me as he was telling the story of James. "Makes you wonder why James wasn't a believer during the lifetime of Jesus," I mused. "What did Jesus do or not do that left James skeptical?"

Licona seemed slightly taken aback. "I have to admit, Lee, that has bothered me over the years," he said, his voice taking on a more personal tone. "It still bothers me some, to be honest with you. If the virgin birth really occurred, then how could Jesus' brothers not have believed in him? I'm sure they would have heard it from Mary. Sincerely, I have really struggled with that.

"I mentioned this recently to a friend who is somewhat of a skeptic, and he surprised me by saying, 'It doesn't bother me at all. If I had a brother who was perfect, even if he had been born of a virgin, I'd hate him, and I just wouldn't follow him.' That was interesting to me. But honestly, we don't really know, historically speaking. As resurrection scholar William Lane Craig asks, 'What would it take to convince *you* that your brother is the Lord?' Really, the only thing that could account for that would be what's reported in the early creed: That the crucified Jesus appeared alive to James."

With that, Licona advanced to the last of his minimal facts.

FACT #5: JESUS' TOMB WAS EMPTY

"Although the fifth fact—that the tomb of Jesus was empty—is part of the minimal case for the resurrection, it doesn't enjoy the nearly universal scholarly consensus that the first four do," Licona began. "Still, there's strong evidence in its favor. Historian Gary Habermas has determined that about 75 percent of scholars on the subject regard it as a historical fact. That's quite a large majority.

"Basically, there are three strands of evidence for it: The Jerusalem factor, the enemy attestation, and the testimony of women."

"Jerusalem factor?" I asked. "What's that?"

"This refers to the fact that Jesus was publicly executed and buried in Jerusalem, and then his resurrection was proclaimed in the very same city. In fact, several weeks after the crucifixion, Peter declared to a crowd right there in Jerusalem, 'God has raised this Jesus to life, and we are all witnesses of the fact.'[56] Frankly, it would have been impossible for Christianity to get off the ground in Jerusalem if Jesus' body were still in the tomb. The Roman or Jewish authorities could have simply gone over to his tomb, viewed his corpse, and the misunderstanding would have been over. But there's no indication that this occurred.

"Instead, what we do hear is enemy attestation to the empty tomb. In other words, what were the skeptics saying? That the disciples stole the body. This is reported not only by Matthew, but also by Justin Martyr and Tertullian. Here's the thing:

Why would you say someone stole the body if it were still in the tomb? This is an implicit admission that the tomb was empty.

"I've got a 12-year-old son. If he went into school and said, 'The dog ate my homework,' he would be implicitly admitting he doesn't have his homework to turn in. Likewise, you wouldn't claim that the disciples stole the body if it were still in his tomb. It's an indirect admission that the body was unavailable for display. There's no way Jesus' enemies would have admitted this if it weren't true. On top of that, the idea that the disciples stole the body is a lame explanation. Are we supposed to believe they conspired to steal the body, pulled it off, and then were willing to suffer continuously and even die for what they knew was a lie? That's such an absurd idea that scholars universally reject it today.

"In addition, we have the testimony of women that the tomb was empty. Not only were women the first to discover the vacant grave, but they are mentioned in all four Gospels, whereas male witnesses appear only later and in just two of them."

"Why is this important?"

"Because in both first-century Jewish and Roman cultures, women were lowly esteemed and their testimony was considered questionable. They were certainly considered less credible than men. For example, the Jewish Talmud says, 'Sooner let the words of the Law be burnt than delivered to women,'[57] and 'Any evidence which a woman [gives] is not valid [to offer], also they are not valid to offer.'[58] Josephus said, 'But let not the testimony of women be admitted, on account of the levity and boldness of their sex.'[59]

"My point is this: If you were going to concoct a story in an effort to fool others, then you would never, in that day, hurt your own credibility by saying women discovered the empty tomb. It would be extremely unlikely that the Gospel writers would invent testimony like this because they wouldn't get any mileage out of it. In fact, it could hurt them. If they'd felt the freedom simply to make things up, surely they'd claim that men—maybe Peter or John or even Joseph of Arimathea—were the first to find the tomb empty. The best theory for why the Gospel writers would include such an embarrassing detail is because that's what actually happened and they were committed to recording it accurately, regardless of the credibility problem it created in that culture.

I interrupted. "Let's put this into context, though: An empty tomb doesn't prove the resurrection."

"Granted, but remember that this is just one of the five minimal facts. And it's entirely in line with the beliefs of the disciples, Paul, and James that Jesus rose from the dead, since a resurrection implies an empty tomb."

A RESTRAINED CONCLUSION

Licona summarized, "So we've looked at relevant sources, and we've applied responsible historical methodology. Now we need restrained results. We have to ask ourselves: What's the best explanation for the evidence—the explanation that doesn't leave out any of the facts or strain to make anything fit? My conclusion, based on the evidence, is that Jesus did return from the dead."

"You personally think the case is strong?"

"Oh, absolutely. No other explanation comes close to accounting for all the facts. Historically speaking, I think we've got a cogent and convincing case."

Licona could have presented all kinds of historical evidence for the resurrection, but instead he limited himself to only five facts that are extremely well-attested historically and that the vast majority of scholars—including skeptics—concede are trustworthy. I was impressed that he didn't merely throw around hyperbolic affirmations for the resurrection from conservative Christians who only considered the evidence that was in favor of their cherished doctrine. Making his case from the lips of liberal and disbelieving scholars served greatly to heighten the credibility of the Easter event.

As Licona finished his presentation and relaxed back into the couch, I thumbed through the notes attached to the clipboard on my lap. Having studied the most current—and most compelling—objections of Muslims, atheists, and other resurrection doubters, and having personally questioned other opponents to Jesus' bodily return from the grave, I knew there was another side to the story. How strong was it? How would Licona respond? Would his evidence emerge unscathed or disintegrate under scrutiny?

"Let's grab some lunch," I suggested as I stood and stretched. "Then we'll see how well your case stands up to cross-examination."

THE QUR'AN VERSUS THE BIBLE

Since Licona had started his case with the crucifixion of Jesus— confidently declaring that it was "as solid as anything in ancient history"—I decided to begin there once we had finished eating. After all, I mused, the more than one billion Muslims in the world would adamantly disagree with Licona's assertion.

I picked up my well-worn copy of the Qur'an from the coffee table. "You say Jesus was killed by crucifixion; but on the contrary, Muslims believe Jesus never really died on the cross," I said. Finding the Fourth Surah, I read aloud verses 157 and 158:

> That they said (in boast), "We killed Christ Jesus the son of Mary, the Messenger of Allah.";—but they killed him not, nor crucified him, but so it was made to appear to them, and those who differ therein are full of doubts, with no (certain) knowledge, but only conjecture to follow, for of a surety they killed him not:—Nay, Allah raised him up unto Himself; and Allah is Exalted in Power, Wise.[60]

I closed the book and continued. "There seem to be two possibilities: Either someone was made to look like Jesus, and the Romans killed that person. Or Jesus was on the cross, but Allah made it appear that he'd died when he really didn't. Then they put him in a tomb, Allah healed him, and Jesus was taken to heaven. Aren't those possible scenarios?"

Licona's posture straightened. "Well, anything is possible with God," he said, "but the real question is where does the evidence point? In other words, the question doesn't concern what God *can do*, but what God *did*. And the Qur'an is not a very credible source when it comes to Jesus."

"You don't believe the Qur'an has good credentials?"

"The Qur'an provides a test for people to verify its divine origin: Gather the wisest people in the world and call upon the *jinn*, which are similar to demons but without all of the negative connotations, and try to write a surah, or chapter, that's as good as one in the Qur'an. The implication, of course, is that this can't be done."

"Do you think it can be?"

"I think so, rather easily. Someone else might disagree. And that points out the basic problem with that kind of test of authenticity: It really comes down to what sounds best to you, sort of like choosing between McDonald's and Burger King. It's very subjective, don't you think? That's why it's not a good test of the Qur'an's divine nature.

"In contrast, Jesus provided a historical event—his resurrection—as the test by which we can know his message is true. Now, that's a good test, because a resurrection isn't going to happen unless God does it."

THE ISLAMIC CATCH-22

I agreed with Licona—the supposed lyrical quality of the Qur'an was unavoidably a subjective test. "That's why you don't believe the Qur'an is credible?" I asked.

"That's only the beginning of the Qur'an's problems when it comes to Jesus," Licona said. "On top of that, you've got the Islamic Catch-22."

"The what?"

"Let me explain it," he replied. "We can establish historically that Jesus predicted his own imminent and violent death."

"How so?" I asked.

"We find this reported in Mark, which is the earliest Gospel, and it's also attested in a number of other literary forms, which is really strong evidence in the eyes of historians. Also, a lot of times when Jesus predicts his death, the disciples say, 'No, this can't happen,' or they don't understand. This makes them look like knuckleheads, so it's embarrassing to the disciples, who are the leaders of the church, to put this in the Gospel. This indicates that this is authentic because you certainly wouldn't make up something that puts the apostles in a bad light. Consequently, there are good historical reasons for believing Jesus did actually predict his imminent and violent demise."

"Okay, I think that's pretty clear," I said. "But where does the Islamic Catch-22 come in?"

"If Jesus did *not* die a violent and imminent death, then that makes him a false prophet. But the Qur'an says he's a great prophet, and so the Qur'an would be wrong and thus discredited. On the other hand, if Jesus *did* die a violent and imminent death as he predicted, then he is indeed a great prophet—but this would contradict the Qur'an, which says he didn't die on the cross. So either way, the Qur'an is discredited.

"The bottom line is this: Unless you're a Muslim who is already committed to the Qur'an, no historian worth his salt would ever place the Qur'an as a more credible source on Jesus over the New Testament, which has four biographies and other writings dated shortly after the time of Jesus and which contains eyewitness testimony. In historical Jesus studies, I don't know of a single scholar who consults the Qur'an as a source on the historical Jesus."

"But you have to admit," I said, "that it would be hard to prove or disprove whether Allah substituted somebody else on the cross at the last minute."

"Listen, I could come up with a theory that says we were all created just five minutes ago with food in our stomachs from meals we never ate and memories of events that never took place. How would you disprove that? But the question is: Where does the evidence point? What seems to be the most rational belief? Again, unless you're a Muslim who already is so predisposed to believing Islamic doctrines that you can't look at the data objectively in any sense, no one would say the Qur'an is a credible source when it comes to Jesus."

DIVINE DECEIVER?

"When I heard a Muslim debate this issue, he took the approach that Jesus was on the cross and that Allah made him appear to be dead, even though he wasn't," I said. "Then he claimed Allah healed Jesus."

"That creates another problem," Licona replied. "Wouldn't this make Allah a deceiver? We could understand it if he deceived his enemies who were trying to kill Jesus. But since we can know historically that Jesus' disciples sincerely believed that he'd been killed and that his corpse had been transformed into an immortal body, this makes God a deceiver of his followers as well. If Jesus never clarified matters with his disciples, then he deceived them, too. Why would you deceive your followers if you knew this was going to spawn a new but false religion? And if God deceived his first-century followers, whom the Qur'an refers to as 'Muslims,' then how can today's Muslims be confident that he's not deceiving them now?"

I found Licona's logic convincing. Simply applying the tools of modern historical scholarship quickly disqualifies the Qur'an as a trustworthy text about Jesus, if for no other reason than the book's late dating. Scholars quibble over a difference of just a few years in the dating of the New Testament, whereas the Qur'an didn't come until *six centuries* after the life of Christ. I also knew, however, that the Qur'an isn't the only book claiming that Jesus didn't die on the cross.

I picked up a copy of the 2006 *New York Times* bestseller *The Jesus Papers* from the couch next to me. Opening it, I got ready to question Licona about its eye-opening allegations that seek to refute the crucifixion.

PILATE'S HIDDEN AGENDA

"Michael Baigent claims in The Jesus Papers that although the Jewish Zealots wanted Jesus crucified, Pontius Plate was conflicted because Jesus had been telling people to pay their taxes to Rome," I said as I flipped to page 125. Then I read to Licona the text I'd highlighted in yellow:

> Pilate was Rome's official representative in Judea, and Rome's main argument with the Jews was that they declined to pay their tax to Caesar. Yet here was a leading Jew—the legitimate king no less—telling his people to pay the tax. How could Pilate try, let alone condemn, such a man who, on the face of it, was supporting Roman policy? Pilate would himself be charged with dereliction of duty should he proceed with the condemnation of such a supporter.[61]

"And so," I continued, "Baigent says Pilate decided to condemn Jesus to please the crowd, but he took steps to ensure Jesus would survive so he wouldn't have to report to Rome that he'd killed him. After all, Mike, you've already conceded that it's possible to survive a crucifixion, and Baigent speculates that Jesus had been given medication to induce the appearance of death. In fact, the Gospels indicate Jesus died pretty quickly.

"Set aside the issue of Baigent's credibility for a moment," I said. "Let's just deal with the theory he offers. Doesn't this undermine your claim that Jesus died on the cross?"

Licona sighed. "Honestly, Lee, this is just so weak," he said. "First, Baigent claims that aloes or myrrh were used to revive Jesus after his ordeal on the cross. If these common herbs could be used to resuscitate and bring back to health a crucified individual who had been horribly scourged, then why in the world aren't we using them today?" he asked, his tone indignant. "Why aren't hospitals using them? They would be wonder drugs! Come on—that's ridiculous!"

Now he was on a roll. "And the idea that Rome would never crucify someone who was supporting them just flies in the face of the facts. Look at Paul—he urged people to obey the governing authorities because God has placed them in charge, yet that didn't stop Rome from executing him!

"Think about it: If Jesus survived the crucifixion, he'd be horribly mutilated and limping. How would that convince the disciples that he's the risen Prince of Life? That's absurd. Baigent has nothing to back up his wild claims. Look at the writings on the resurrection by legitimate scholars over the past 20 years: Only about one in a thousand even suggests it's possible that Jesus survived the crucifixion. There's a tidal wave of scholarship on the other side. This is almost in the same category as denying the Holocaust!"

I jumped in. "Baigent claims the Bible itself backs up his theory," I pointed out. "He says that in the Gospel of Mark, when Joseph of Arimathea requests Jesus' body from Pilate, he uses the Greek word *soma*, which denotes a living body. In reply, Pilate uses the word *ptoma* for body, which means a corpse. Says Baigent: 'In other words, the Greek text of Mark's Gospel is making it clear that while Joseph is asking for the living body of Jesus, Pilate grants him what he believes to be the corpse. *Jesus' survival is revealed right there in the actual Gospel account.*'[62]

Licona shook his head in disbelief. "That's pure rubbish," he said with disdain.

I pointed at him. "Prove it," I said.

"Okay," he said, picking up the challenge. "The truth is

that the word *soma* makes no distinction between a living or a dead body. In fact, in Acts 9:36-37 Luke talks about the death of Tabitha. After she dies, he says they washed her *soma*, or her body. Obviously, it's a corpse. Luke 17:37 says, 'Where there is a dead body, there the vultures will gather.' Again, the word he uses is *soma*. There's example after example, even in Josephus, of *soma* meaning "corpse." So Baigent doesn't know what he's talking about here, either.

"What's more, Baigent is ignoring the context in Mark. The Gospel makes it clear that Jesus was dead. Mark 15:37 says 'Jesus breathed his last'; in Mark 15:45, eyewitnesses confirmed Jesus was dead; and in Mark 15:47–16:1, Mary Magdalene and the other women watch Jesus being buried and return on Sunday morning to anoint him. They surely thought he was dead. So there's nothing at all to support Baigent's claims."

There was no need to go further: Baigent's case would be instantly dismissed by any impartial judge. Licona's first fact—that Jesus was killed by crucifixion—remained unrefuted by any credible counterargument.

Before we moved on, however, I wanted to ask Licona about his opinion on popular writers like Baigent whose authentic-sounding theories often confuse readers unfamiliar with the other side of the story. "Does it bother you that Baigent's book was a bestseller and that thousands of people may believe it's true?" I asked.

"What it shows," said Licona, "is that people are not only willing to believe this sort of nonsense, but that Western culture is looking for a justification for an alternative to the traditional view of Christianity."

"Why do you think that's the case?"

"There are numerous reasons. Sometimes it's moral issues,"

came his response. "They don't want to be constrained by the traditional Jesus, who calls them to a life of holiness. One friend of mine finally acknowledged that Jesus rose from the dead, but he still won't become a Christian because he said he wanted to be the master of his own life—that's exactly how he put it. So in many cases—not all—it's a heart issue, not a head issue.

"Some people just don't like what Jesus is demanding of them."

HALLUCINATIONS AND DELUSIONS

So far, I felt Licona had adequately responded to my challenges to Fact #1: That Jesus really died. But did Jesus actually appear to people after his death? Atheist Richard Carrier doesn't think so:

> I believe the best explanation, consistent with both scientific findings and the surviving evidence...is that the first Christians experienced hallucinations of the risen Christ, of one form or another....In the ancient world, to experience supernatural manifestations of ghosts, gods and wonders was not only accepted, but often encouraged.[63]

"Doesn't this," I pressed Licona, "neatly account for the appearances of Jesus?"

"Actually," he said, "if all we had was Jesus appearing to Peter, then maybe I'd buy into the hallucination theory."

That admission startled me. "You would?" I asked.

"*Maybe*," Licona stressed. "He's grieving, he's full of anxiety—*maybe*."

That seemed like a significant concession to me. But Licona wasn't finished. "But that's not all we have," he continued. "We've not only got multiple appearances to individuals, but also at least three appearances to groups of people. And a group of people isn't going to hallucinate the same thing at the same time."

"Can you back that up?"

"I lived in Virginia Beach for 14 years. Half the Navy SEALs are stationed there, and I got to know a number of them. To become a SEAL, they have to go through 'hell week.' They start on a Sunday night and they go through Friday, during which they get maybe three to five hours of sleep the whole time. They're being barked at continually, there's high stress, they're constantly exercising, and inevitably fatigue and sleep deprivation set in.

"About 80 percent of the guys hallucinate due to the lack of sleep. A lot of times they're out on a raft doing an exercise called 'around the world,' where they go out in the ocean, around a buoy, and head back to shore. They're trying to be the first to return because then they'll be rewarded with rest. It's during this time that many start seeing things.

"One SEAL told me he actually believed he saw an octopus come out of the water and wave at him. Another guy believed a train was coming across the water toward his raft. He'd point to it, and the others would say, 'Are you crazy? There are no trains out here in the ocean.' He believed it so strongly, in fact, that before what he perceived as the train could hit him, he rolled into the ocean, and the others had to retrieve him from the water.

"A SEAL told me about another guy who was wildly waving his oars in the air. When he was asked what he was doing, he said, 'I'm trying to hit the dolphins that are jumping over the boat.'

"I asked the SEAL, 'Did you see the dolphins?'

"He said, 'No.'

"I said, 'Did anyone else see the dolphins?'

"He said, 'No, they were busy having their own hallucinations!'

"You see, hallucinations aren't contagious. They're personal. They're like dreams. I couldn't wake up my wife in the middle of the night and say, 'Honey, I'm dreaming of being in Hawaii. Quick, go back to sleep, join me in my dream, and we'll have a free vacation.' You can't do that. Scientists will tell you hallucinations are the same way.

"We've got at least three group appearances, so the hallucination theory doesn't work. On top of that, hallucinations can't account for the empty tomb. They can't account for Jesus' appearance to Paul because he wasn't grieving—he was trying to destroy the church. And in the midst of that mission, Paul believed he saw the risen Jesus. And James was a skeptic; he wasn't in the frame of mind for hallucinations to occur, either."

I knew Licona's analysis of the hallucination theory was solid. According to psychologist Gary Collins, who was a university professor for more than two decades, who authored dozens of books on psychology, and who was the president of the American Association of Christian Counselors:

> Hallucinations are individual occurrences. By their
> very nature only one person can see a given hallucina-
> tion at a time. They certainly aren't something which
> can be seen by a group of people. Neither is it possible
> that one person could somehow induce a hallucina-

tion in somebody else. Since a hallucination exists only in the subjective, personal sense, it is obvious that others cannot witness it.[64]

I decided to try another approach. "What about the idea that 'groupthink' could have taken over in those groups?" I asked. "Maybe people were suggestible and perhaps talked into seeing a vision."

"At best, that would account for only the disciples' belief that they'd seen the risen Jesus. It wouldn't account for the empty tomb because if they were seeing only a vision, then the actual body should still be in there. It wouldn't account for the conversion of Paul, since it's unlikely an opponent would be susceptible to groupthink. Same with the skeptic James. In fact, with the crucifixion of Jesus, James was probably all the more convinced that Jesus was a failed messiah because he was hung on the tree and cursed by God."[65]

I wasn't ready to give up yet. "If these weren't technically hallucinations, could these people have been deluded?" I asked. "You know, like Marshall Applewhite of the Heaven's Gate cult who committed suicide with more than three dozen of his followers because they believed a spaceship hiding behind the comet Hale-Bopp would pick them up."

"You're right—hallucinations and delusions aren't the same," Licona said. "A hallucination is a false perception of something that's not there; a delusion is when someone persists in a belief after receiving conclusive evidence to the contrary. In the case of Applewhite, his followers were delusional. They persisted in their belief that they were seeing a spaceship behind the comet even after astronomers assured them they were actually seeing Mars."

"Well, then," I said, "we could postulate the theory that Peter saw a hallucination of Jesus and then he convinced the other disciples—he deluded them—into believing Jesus had risen from the dead."

"Sorry," came the reply. "That doesn't account for all the facts. For example, it doesn't account for the empty tomb because the body would still be there, right? And it wouldn't account for the conversion of Paul. Listen—you weren't sucked in by a cult, were you, Lee? Most people weren't. Paul, who was actively opposing the church, wasn't going to get sucked into believing Jesus had returned from the dead, and neither was James. At best, the delusion theory could only conceivably account for why some of the disciples believed; it doesn't account for most of the facts. So therefore it's not a good historical theory."

Deftly, using evidence and logic, Licona had deflected the biggest objections to the appearances of the risen Jesus that have been promoted by critics in recent years. And his second, third, and fourth "minimal facts"—that Jesus' disciples, the persecutor Paul, and the skeptic James believed they'd encountered the risen Jesus—appeared to survive intact.

Still, there was one remaining minimal fact that I wanted to challenge: the burial place of Jesus. Was his tomb empty on the first Easter—and why?

PAUL AND THE EMPTY TOMB

I began addressing the issue of the empty tomb by recapping the argument that Richard Carrier and Uta Ranke-Heinemann, a professor of the history of religion at the University of Essen in Germany, use to try to account for it.

"According to Carrier," I said, "Paul didn't believe in an empty tomb because he believed Jesus had a spiritual body, which is why he never mentions the empty tomb. Later, Mark made up the empty tomb story—for him, it wasn't historical but symbolic, representing Jesus being freed from his corpse. According to Carrier, Jesus' body was the empty tomb. Then legendary embellishment took over in Matthew, Luke, and John.[66]

"As for Ranke-Heinemann, she says the empty tomb's legendary nature is proven because Paul, 'the most crucial preacher of Christ's resurrection and the earliest New Testament writer besides, says nothing about it. As far as Paul is concerned, it doesn't exist.'"[67]

Skeptic Gerd Lüdemann agrees: "If [Paul] had known about the empty tomb, he would certainly have referred to it in order to have an additional argument for the resurrection."[68]

With that background, I said to Licona, "You believe the empty tomb is important enough to be included in your five minimal facts, right?"

"That's right," he said.

"Then if it's important in building *your* case for the resurrection, why wouldn't it be equally important for Paul in building *his* case?" I asked. "Why wouldn't Paul have stressed it every bit as much as you did when he was trying to convince others that the resurrection was true?"

Licona looked a little perplexed that this issue was even coming up. "I don't think he had to," came his reply. "It is like when you say a baby died of Sudden Infant Death Syndrome. No one has to speak about an empty crib. It's clearly implied.

"The ancient meaning of *resurrection* was the bringing back of a corpse to life and transforming it into an immortal body. Imagine saying to Paul, 'If you believed in an empty tomb, why didn't you mention it?' Paul would have said, 'Well, what do you think I meant when I said *resurrection*? You want me to spell it out for you? Of course, I mean an empty tomb!'"

"But can you blame people today for wishing Paul had been more explicit?" I asked.

Licona shrugged. "Maybe the skeptics want to have it spelled out for them in the twenty-first century, but Paul was writing this in the first century. They all knew what resurrection meant. To them, Paul was plenty explicit. He's clear in his own letters. Moreover, when Luke reports Paul stating in Acts 13:37 that Jesus' body 'did not see decay,' readers surely understood that his physical body had been raised. And if the body was raised, then the tomb was empty. This is early apostolic tradition."

In the end, I had to admit: This made sense.

THE "RELOCATION HYPOTHESIS"

I moved on to another current objection to the empty tomb: the "relocation hypothesis" championed by skeptics James Tabor and Jeffery Jay Lowder, whose attacks on the resurrection have proven popular on the Internet.

According to Lowder, "Jesus' body was stored (but not buried) in Joseph's tomb Friday before sunset and moved on Saturday night to a second tomb in the graveyard of the condemned, where Jesus was buried dishonorably."[69] Tabor asserts that someone—probably members of Jesus' own family—removed the body from his "temporary grave" and reburied him elsewhere.

I was curious how Licona would respond. "What's your reaction?" I asked. "Does their theory pass muster as a historical hypothesis?"

"No, it doesn't," he answered.

"Why not?"

"Here's the question we have to ask: Does it account for all the facts and do so without straining? At best, all it accounts for is the empty tomb. And interestingly, the empty tomb didn't convince any of the disciples—with the possible exception of John—that Jesus had returned from the dead. It was the appearances of Jesus that convinced them, and the reburial theory can't account for these.

"It's like with David Koresh in the 1990s. He predicted that when he died he would rise from the dead three years later. Well, he didn't. But let's suppose three years after the date of his death at Waco, some Branch Davidians said, 'Hey, Koresh is back to life again.' You go and check for his remains at the coroner's office, and they're missing. Would you, as a Christian, abandon your faith and become a Branch Davidian because of that? Of course not. You'd say, 'Come on, the remains were moved, stolen, or misplaced.'

"Think about it: Why did Paul move from skepticism to faith? He said it was the appearances that led to his faith. The same with James. The appearances were the key—and, again, this relocation theory fails to account for them.

"Besides, on a more mundane note, if the family moved the body, don't you think somebody would have said something to straighten out the disciples when they were going around proclaiming a resurrection? And remember: The explanation for the empty tomb that was circulating at the time was that the disciples had stolen the body. If the body had merely been relocated, why didn't somebody in authority point that out so they could squelch the Christian movement in its infancy?"

PRODUCING JESUS' BODY

One way Christians often defend the empty tomb is to say that if the grave still contained Jesus' body, then the authorities could have paraded it down Main Street in Jerusalem and thus killed the developing Christian movement. Licona was using a similar argument.

But is that really true? After all, the disciples' public proclamation about the resurrection came some seven weeks after the crucifixion, when Peter declared to a crowd of several thousand people in Jerusalem: "God has raised this Jesus to life, and we are all witnesses of the fact."[70]

Skeptic Robert Price suggests the disciples were "shrewd enough" to wait this long so that "disconfirmation had become impossible." He said that after 50 days it would have been pointless to produce the remains of Jesus.[71]

"The body would have been far too decomposed to be identified without modern forensics," agreed Lowder.[72]

Licona was incredulous. "Price thinks the disciples were being *shrewd* to wait until the corpse was unrecognizable?" he asked. "They were laying their lives on the line! Why would they plot and scheme this way so their reward would be continual suffering, even to the point of death? That doesn't add up."

"What about recognizing the body?" I asked.

It turned out Licona had already done some investigation into the issue of how long a corpse could be identified. "I talked to three coroners from Louisiana, Virginia, and California about whether a body would be recognizable after 50 days," he said. "All agreed that even in a humid climate, you'd still be able to recognize a body somewhat—at least in stature, the hair, and possibly the wounds.

"Now, had people been able to go back to Jesus' tomb after 50 days and had they seen a severely decomposed body of the same stature as Jesus, with the same hair, and possibly even wounds consistent with scourging and crucifixion, then enough doubt would have been put into enough minds that subsequent Christian apologists would have had to address why there was a great exodus of believers at that point. But we have no record of any such thing.

"In other words, if the authorities had claimed this was Jesus, then the burden of proof would have shifted. The onus would have been on the disciples to disprove it. Nobody needed to see all Jesus' facial features; merely producing a severely decomposed body from the right tomb and with the right stature and hair type would have put the disciples on the defensive. Their movement would have been greatly undermined. But of course, there's absolutely no historical evidence to suggest this happened."

EVIDENCE THAT CONVINCES

"What about you personally?" I asked. "Are you at the point where you never doubt anymore?"

Licona was candid. "I still have periods when I experience some doubt—in a way, that's my personality," he said. "Sometimes I still wonder, 'Am I looking at these arguments as objectively as I can?' I'm always trying to neutralize my biases. When someone raises an objection, most of the time I'm not trying to think of a refutation. I'm trying to understand and internalize the argument—to grant it its full weight. I try to feel it the same way it's being felt by the person who holds it. And that will cause some doubts because I'm sort of experiencing what the other person is experiencing."

"What do you do then?"

"I look at the data. I try to apply responsible historical methodology," he said. "And I always come back to the resurrection."

Over and over, Michael Licona ultimately finds it convincing: A very real event of history that validates the divinity of the real Jesus.

BRIDGING THE GAP

The reality of the resurrection, which transformed skeptics like Paul and James in the first century, continues to radically redirect lives today—even those of tough-minded scientists.

For example, few researchers in America have achieved the professional acclaim of Francis S. Collins. As a medical doctor with a doctorate in chemistry, he was appointed by President Bill Clinton to head the Human Genome Project (HGP) in 1993; and by the year 2003, HGP had successfully decoded the three billion genes of human DNA. Collins also helped discover the genetic anomalies that lead to cystic fibrosis, neurofibromatosis, and Huntington's disease. I've had the pleasure of exchanging emails with him from time to time.

For much of his early life, Collins was an atheist who looked at Jesus as "a myth, a fairy tale, a superhero in a bedtime story." Then the faith of some of his desperately ill patients prompted him to investigate spiritual issues. Turning to history, he was amazed at the evidence for Jesus of Nazareth. The four Gospels, he found, were written within decades of Jesus' death. They were clearly rooted in the testimony of eyewitnesses. They'd been passed down through the centuries with great fidelity. And, of course, they describe Jesus rising bodily from the dead.

Can a rational scientist believe in such "nonsense"? This was, conceded Collins, "difficult stuff." In the end, though, came this epiphany: "If Christ really was the Son of God, as he explicitly claimed, then surely of all those who had ever walked the earth, he could suspend the laws of nature if he needed to do so to achieve a more important purpose."

For Collins, this was more than just a historical curiosity. "The crucifixion and resurrection also provided something else," he said in his 2006 bestseller *The Language of God.*

"My desire to draw close to God was blocked by my own pride and sinfulness, which in turn was an inevitable consequence of my own selfish desire to be in control," he said. "Now the crucifixion and resurrection emerged as the compelling solution to the gap that yawned between God and myself, a gap that could now be bridged by the person of Jesus Christ."[73]

That is what the real—and resurrected—Jesus does.

Christianity's Beliefs about Jesus Were Copied from Pagan Religions

A s a young reporter at the *Chicago Tribune*, I watched in sympathy as a heartbreaking spectacle unfolded in the newsroom. The editor received an anonymous envelope containing a recent column by an up-and-coming *Tribune* writer, as well as a photocopy of an article written eight years earlier by Pete Hamill of the *New York Post* and reprinted in a collection of his works.

The theme of the article and substantial parts of the language were virtually identical, resulting in a charge of plagiarism—a humiliating and career-stunting allegation that led to the reporter's suspension for a month without pay. Later, the editor discovered that the writer was involved in other unethical behavior, and the young columnist resigned.

Through the years, allegations of plagiarism have created problems for lots of journalists, scholars, politicians, and students—even a young Helen Keller.[74] It's a serious and escalating problem at universities, as the Internet has made cut-and-paste plagiarism much easier for students who are facing imminent deadlines for term papers. And plenty of Web sites offer papers and projects that students can buy and pass off as their own. In response, oth-

er Internet entrepreneurs have created Web-based resources that help professors detect previously published material.

Technically, it's not a crime to commit plagiarism, but it's a serious civil and ethical offense to claim another person's words or literary concepts as your own. Most of the time, the penalties are informal but nevertheless devastating: A failing grade, a destroyed career, and an embarrassing loss of credibility.

In a similar way, a recent wave of books has claimed that Christianity's key tenets about Jesus—including his virgin birth and resurrection—aren't historical truths, but rather plagiarized ideas taken from earlier "mystery religions" that flourished in the Mediterranean world. The allegation that Christianity is merely a "copycat" religion—one that recycles elements from ancient mythology—has, for many people, destroyed its credibility.

"Nothing in Christianity is original." That line is among the most famous in one of publishing's greatest success stories, *The Da Vinci Code*. The book charges that everything of importance in Christianity, from Communion to Jesus' birthday to Sunday worship, was "taken directly from earlier pagan mystery religions."

At first blush, the parallels between the story of Jesus and the myths of ancient gods appear to be striking. For instance, writers have said that the pre-Christian god Mithras was born of a virgin in a cave on December 25; was considered a great traveling teacher; had 12 disciples; promised his followers immortality; sacrificed himself for world peace; was buried in a tomb and rose again three days later; instituted a Eucharist or "Lord's Supper"; and was considered the Logos, the Redeemer, the Messiah, and "the Way, the Truth, and the Life." Sound familiar?

If these allegations are true, then the so-called "real Jesus" has no more authority than an imaginary "sun god" worshiped by primitive tribes millennia ago. If his life, teachings, and resurrection are little more than echoes of mythological characters, then there'd be no good reason to follow, worship, or rely on Jesus. He becomes as useless as the make-believe Zeus, as irrelevant as the long-forgotten Mithras.

But are these charges accurate? To find out, I decided to focus initially on the allegation that Jesus' resurrection—the pivotal event that Christians say confirmed his deity—was essentially plagiarized from earlier pagan stories. Among those giving credence to that theory is Tim Callahan, religion editor of *Skeptic* magazine. "The possible influences on the Jews that might have produced a belief in resurrection are the myriad fertility cults among all the peoples of the ancient world," he says.[78]

I raised this issue with Michael Licona. He'd been an excellent guide through my other questions about the resurrection, and he'd also coauthored the award-winning book *The Case for the Resurrection of Jesus*. Surely he'd looked into the idea that the resurrection was a story copied from other religions.

A NEARLY UNIVERSAL CONSENSUS

"Why," I asked Licona, "should the story of Jesus' resurrection have any more credibility than pagan stories of dying and rising gods—such as Osiris, Adonis, Attis, and Marduk—that are so obviously mythological?"

Licona was indeed well-versed on this controversy. "First of all, it's important to understand that these claims don't in any way negate the good historical evidence we have for Jesus' resurrection, which I spelled out in our earlier discussion," he pointed out. "You can't dismiss the resurrection unless you can refute its solid core of supporting evidence."[79]

I agreed that was an important piece of this puzzle to keep in mind—and one that "copycat" theorists typically forget.

"Second, T. N. D. Mettinger—a senior Swedish scholar, professor at Lund University, and member of the Royal Academy of Letters, History, and Antiquities of Stockholm—wrote one of the most recent academic treatments of dying and rising gods in antiquity. He admits in his book *The Riddle of Resurrection* that the consensus among modern scholars—*nearly universal*—is that there were no dying and rising gods that preceded Christianity. They all post-dated the first century."

Obviously, that timing is absolutely crucial: Christianity couldn't have borrowed the idea of the resurrection if myths about dying and rising gods weren't even circulating when Christianity was birthed in the first century.

"Then Mettinger said he was going to take exception to that nearly universal scholarly conviction," Licona continued. "He takes a decidedly minority position and claims there are at least three—and possibly as many as five—dying and rising gods that predate Christianity. But the key question is this: Are there any actual parallels between these myths and Jesus' resurrection?"

"What did Mettinger conclude?" I asked.

"In the end, after combing through all of these accounts and critically analyzing them, Mettinger adds that none of these serve as parallels to Jesus. *None* of them," Licona emphasized.

"They are far different from the reports of Jesus rising from the dead. They occurred in the unspecified and distant past and were usually related to the seasonal life-and-death cycle of vegetation. In contrast, Jesus' resurrection isn't repeated, isn't related to changes in the seasons, and was sincerely believed to be an actual event by those who lived in the same generation of the historical Jesus. In addition, Mettinger concludes that 'there is no evidence for the death of the dying and rising gods as vicarious suffering for sins.'"[80]

I later got Mettinger's book to double-check Licona's account of his research. Sure enough, Mettinger caps his study with this stunning statement: "There is, as far as I am aware, no *prima facie* [at first sight, obvious] evidence that the death and resurrection of Jesus is a mythological construct, drawing on the myths and rites of the dying and rising gods of the surrounding world."[81]

In short, this leading scholar's analysis is a sharp rebuke of authors and Internet bloggers who make grand claims about the pagan origins of Jesus' return from the dead. Ultimately, Mettinger affirmed, "The death and resurrection of Jesus retains its unique character in the history of religions."[82]

BOWLING IN HEAVEN

Mettinger's assessment was extremely significant, but I wanted to dig deeper into the mythology. "Do I understand correctly that these ancient myths were used to try to explain why things died in the fall and came back in the spring?" I asked.

"Yes, things like that," Licona replied. "When I was a kid, I asked my mom, 'What's thunder?' She said, 'It's angels bowling in heaven.' Obviously, that's just a story. Similarly, in ancient Canaan, a kid would ask his mom, 'Why does the rain stop in the summer?' And his mom would tell him the story of Baal."

"Is this one of the myths that Mettinger thinks predates Christianity?" I asked.

"That's right. In one of the more popular stories, Baal is the storm god in heaven. He's responsible for the rain. His nemesis is Mot, who's in the netherworld. One day Mot and Baal are trash-talking each other. Mot says, 'You think you're so tough, Baal? You leave behind your clouds and lightning bolts and wind and rain and come on down here—I'll show you who your daddy is.' So Baal leaves everything behind and goes to the underworld—where Mot swallows him. How do we know this? It stopped raining!

"Later, Baal's mother goes down and tells Mot, 'Let my son go!' Mot says, 'No!' So she brutalizes him until he finally says, 'Okay, mercy! Go away and I'll let him go!' She leaves the netherworld, and a couple of months later, Baal's dad says, 'Our son's alive.' How does he know? It's raining again!

"This is like my mom trying to explain thunder to me as a child. They talked about this every year: Baal died and Baal came back. Nobody ever saw it. There were no eyewitnesses. It supposedly occurred in the gray, distant, undated past. It was a fable to explain why there was no rain in the summer—and nothing more. Now, does that sound anything like the resurrection of Jesus? Absolutely not! It's totally different. Jesus' resurrection is supported by strong historical data that is by far best explained by him returning from the dead."

"What about the Egyptian god Osiris?" I asked.

"Osiris is interesting," he said, smiling. "The most popular account says Osiris' brother killed him, chopped him into 14 pieces, and scattered them around the world. Well, the goddess Isis feels compassion for Osiris, so she looks for his body parts in order to give him a proper burial. She finds only 13 of them, she puts them back together, and Osiris is buried. But he doesn't come back to this world; he's given the status of god of the netherworld—a gloomy, shadowy place of semiconsciousness. As a friend of mine says, 'This isn't a resurrection, it's a zombification!' This is no parallel to Jesus' resurrection, for which there is strong historical support."

I spotted an apparent flaw in Licona's reasoning: One of Christianity's earliest apologists, or defenders of the faith, was Justin Martyr, who lived from about AD 100 to 164. In a letter he wrote in about 150, Justin discussed several parallels between Christianity and the rising gods of pagan religions. I pointed this out to Licona and asked, "Isn't that evidence that Christians recognized that Jesus' resurrection was merely a form of mythology?"

Licona was quite familiar with Justin's writings. "First, we have to look at why Justin was writing this. The Romans were severely persecuting Christians, and Justin was telling the emperor, 'Look, you don't persecute people who worship other gods who are similar, so why persecute Christians?' Basically, he was trying to use some arguments to defuse the Roman attacks on the church.

"But look at the parallels he gives. He has to strain to make them. He talks about the sons of Jupiter: Aesculapius was struck by lightning and went to heaven; Bacchus, Hercules, and others rode to heaven on the horse Pegasus. He describes Ariadne and others who 'have been declared to be set among the stars.' He even mentions that when the emperor Augustus was cremated, someone in the crowd swore that he saw his spirit ascending through the flames.

"These aren't resurrections! I know of no highly respected scholar today who'd suggest that these vague fables are parallels to the resurrection of Jesus. We hear this claim only from the hyper-skeptical community on the Internet and books that are marketed to people who lack the background to analyze the facts critically."

Licona's answers had quickly deflated many of the claims I'd heard and read about Jesus' resurrection having been plagiarized from antiquity. I still had questions, however, about the broader implications of the "copycat" allegations. I decided to seek out a leading scholar of ancient history who's also an expert on Mithraism, the "mystery religion" that was once a major rival to Christianity—and, some charge, the source of many of the beliefs Christians took and applied to Jesus.

My trip to picturesque Oxford, Ohio, was almost cancelled because of torrential winter rains. Local rivers were swelling toward flood stage, but I managed to arrive on one of the last flights of the day. The next morning, using an umbrella to shield me, I knocked on the door of an immaculate green house where Edwin Yamauchi lives with his wife, Kimie.

INTERVIEW #4: EDWIN M. YAMAUCHI, PHD

Doctor Yamauchi was born into a Japanese Buddhist family, but he became a Christian in 1952. He has a sterling reputation in the academic world, which is exactly what I needed for this topic where all of these voices of questionable credibility are making truly serious claims. I'd interviewed Yamauchi when I was writing *The Case for Christ,* and I found him to be unassuming, soft-spoken, thorough, and highly credible.

Yamauchi walked me down into his basement, much of which was a warren of bookshelves. We sat at a small table that was partially covered with stacks of papers. I immediately knew why they were there. I'd already told Yamauchi which topics I wanted to cover because I knew he likes to back up his opinions with scholarly articles written by other experts. I could see he was ready for me.

THE MYSTERY RELIGIONS

"Maybe you could start by giving me some background on the mystery religions," I said as we settled in at the table. "When were they popular? What traits did they have in common?"

After taking a sip of his coffee, he replied, "The so-called 'mystery religions' were a variety of religious movements from the eastern Mediterranean that flourished in the early Roman Empire. They offered salvation in a tight-knit community. They were called 'mystery religions' because those who were initiated into them were sworn to secrecy. They had sacred rites, often a common meal, and a special sanctuary."[84]

"Which was the oldest?" I asked.

"That would be the Eleusinian cult of Demeter, which was already established in the Archaic Age of Greece—from 800 to 500 BC. The latest, and certainly the most popular in the later Roman Empire, were the mysteries of Mithras, who started as a Persian fertility god."

Bio: Edwin Yamauchi

- Doctorate in Mediterranean studies from Brandeis University

- Professor at Miami University of Ohio

- Knows 22 languages, including Akkadian, Aramaic, Greek, Hebrew, Chinese, Comanche, Coptic, and Syriac

- Has received eight fellowships from Brandeis, Rutgers, and elsewhere

- Has delivered at scholarly societies 88 papers on Mithraism, Gnosticism, and other topics

- Author of nearly 200 articles and reviews in professional journals

- Lecturer at more than 100 colleges and universities, including Cornell, Princeton, and Yale

- Participant in the first archaeological excavation of the Herodian temple in Jerusalem

- Author of 17 books, including *Persia and the Bible*, *Greece and Babylon*, *Gnostic Ethics and Mandaean Origins*, *The World of the First Christians*, and *Africa and the Bible*

MITHRAISM AND CHRISTIANITY

To make sure we were on the same page, I asked Yamauchi to provide an overview of Mithraic beliefs. He took another drink of coffee before launching into his reply.

"Mithraism was a late Roman mystery religion that was popular among soldiers and merchants. It became a chief rival to Christianity in the first century and later," he said. "The initiates were all men, although one of my students, Jonathan David, recently published a paper arguing that some women may have been involved.[85] The participants met in a cavelike structure called a *mithraeum*, which was centered around a statue of Mithras stabbing a bull."

"How much information about Mithraism exists?"

"There are relatively few texts from the Mithraists themselves. We have some graffiti and inscriptions, as well as descriptions of the religion from its opponents, including Christians. Much of what's been circulated about Mithraism has been based on the theories of a Belgium scholar named Franz Cumont. He was the leading scholar on Mithraism in his day, and he published his famous work *Mysteries of Mithras* in 1903. His work led to speculation that Mithraism had influenced Christianity. Much of what Cumont suggested, however, turned out to be quite unfounded. In the 1970s, scholars at the Second Mythraic Congress in Tehran came to criticize Cumont."

From the papers on the table, Yamauchi dug out a large photograph showing a crowd of scholars at the Congress posing with the empress of Iran on the front steps of a stately building. I surveyed the faces and quickly picked out Yamauchi in the front row.

"Contrary to what Cumont believed, even though Mithras was a Persian god who was attested to as early as the 14th century BC, we have almost no evidence of Mithraism in the sense of a mystery religion in the West until very late—too late to have influenced the beginnings of Christianity. There are a handful of inscriptions that date to the early second century, but the vast majority of texts are dated after AD 140. Most of what we have as evidence of Mithraism comes in the second, third, and fourth centuries AD. That's basically what's wrong with the theories about Mithraism influencing the beginnings of Christianity." (See the "Christianity & Mithraism" timeline.)

"The timing is wrong," I observed.

That was a critically important assessment that would seem to rule out the "copycat" theory.

Yamauchi loaded me down with copies of academic articles and books written by highly regarded scholars who back up that claim. Manfred Clauss, professor of ancient history at Free University in Berlin, wrote in *The Roman Cult of Mithras* that it doesn't make sense to interpret the Mithraic mysteries "as a fore-runner of Christianity."[86] In his book *Mithraism and Christianity*, published by Cambridge University Press, L. Patterson concluded there is "no direct connection between the two religions either in origin or development."[87]

The weight of the evidence was heavy: The claim that Christianity borrowed its central ideas from Mithraism has been thoroughly demolished by a close examination of the dates for when it took root in the West. But what about the numerous parallels between Mithraism and Christianity that popular writers, including novelist Dan Brown, have touted as evidence of Christianity's plagiarism? I was anxious to see how Yamauchi would handle those specific charges.

MITHRAS VERSUS JESUS

I pulled out a list of parallels between Jesus and Mithras. "First, popular writers claim that Mithras was born of a virgin," I said. "Is it true that this was what Mithraism taught?"

Yamauchi looked pained. "No, that's definitely *not* true," he insisted. "He was born out of a rock."

"A rock?"

"Yes, the rock birth is commonly depicted in Mithraic reliefs," he explained. "Mithras emerges fully grown and naked except for a Phrygian cap, and he's holding a dagger and torch. In some variations, flames shoot out from the rock, or he's holding a globe in his hand."

I chuckled. "So unless the rock is considered a virgin, this parallel with Jesus evaporates," I said.

"Entirely correct," he said.

"And that means he wasn't born in a cave, which some writers claim is a second parallel to Christianity."

"Well, it is true that Mithraic sanctuaries were designed to look like caves," Yamauchi said. "Gary Lease discusses that in his study of Mithraism and Christianity."

I later examined Lease's work. He makes the important observation that nowhere in the New Testament is Jesus described as having been born in a cave. This idea is first mentioned in the letter of Barnabas at the beginning of the second century. In fact, Justin Martyr said in the second century that Mithras' cave was a demoniacal imitation of the tradition that Jesus was born in a cave. Lease pointed out, however, that scholar Ernst Benz "has shown conclusively that this Christian tradition does not come from a dependency on Mithraism, but rather from an ages old tradition in Palestine itself of holy shrines in caves." Concluded Lease, "There is no doubt that the Christian tradition does not stem from the Mithraic account."[88]

Returning to my list, I said to Yamauchi, "The third supposed parallel with Jesus is that Mithras was born on December 25."

"Again, that's not a parallel," he replied.

"Why not?"

"Because we don't know the date Jesus was born," he said. "The earliest date celebrated by Christians was January 6—in fact, it's still celebrated by many churches in the East. Of course, December 25 is very close to the winter solstice. This was the date chosen by the emperor Aurelian for the dedication of his temple to Sol Invictus, the god called the 'Unconquerable Sun.' Mithras was closely associated with Sol Invictus; sometimes they're depicted shaking hands. This is apparently how Mithras became associated with December 25."

"When did that date become Christmas for Christians?"

"That seems to be in 336, a year before the death of Constantine, the first Roman emperor to embrace Christianity. We know that before his conversion, he also worshiped Sol Invictus. We know for sure that Constantine made Sunday, or the Lord's Day, an official holiday, even though Christians had already been observing it as the day on which Jesus was resurrected. So it's conceivable that Constantine also appropriated December

25 for the birthday of Christ. We know that instead of simply banning pagan ceremonies, Christian emperors and popes suggested that they appropriate them for Christianity."

"What about the fourth parallel that claims Mithras was a great traveler or master with 12 disciples?"

"No—he was a god, not a teacher," Yamauchi replied, sounding a bit impatient.

"The fifth parallel is that his followers were promised immortality."

"Well, that can be inferred, but certainly that was the hope of most followers of any religion," he said. "So that's not surprising."

"How about the sixth claim, which says Mithras sacrificed himself for world peace?"

Yamauchi sighed. "That's reading Christian theology into something that's not there. He didn't sacrifice himself—he killed a bull."

"The seventh parallel—and one of the most important—is that Mithras was buried in a tomb and rose after three days," I said. "Is there any truth to that?"

"We don't know anything about the death of Mithras," Yamauchi said firmly. "We have a lot of monuments, but we have almost no textual evidence because this was a secret religion. But I know of no references to a supposed death and resurrection."

Indeed, Richard Gordon declared in his authoritative book *Image and Value in the Greco-Roman World* that there is "no death of Mithras"—and thus, there cannot be a resurrection.[90]

I went on, though I had a feeling I could guess his replies.

"Eight, Mithras was considered the Good Shepherd; the Way, the Truth, and the Life; the Logos; the Redeemer; the Savior."

"No. Again, that's reading Christian theology into this."

"Ninth, there was a sacramental meal in Mithraism that paralleled the Lord's Supper."

"Common meals are found in almost all religious communities," he replied. "What is noteworthy is that the Christian apologists Justin Martyr and Tertullian point out the similarities to the Lord's Supper, but they wrote in the second century, long after the Lord's Supper was instituted in Christianity. They claimed the Mithraic meal was a satanic imitation. Clearly, the Christian meal was based on the Passover, not on a mystery religion."

I tossed my list of now-discredited parallels on the table. Amazingly, despite so many writers who've tried to discredit Christianity with such charges of plagiarism, the allegations merely evaporate under scrutiny.

Still, one related issue remained: Whether a gory Mithraic ritual was the source for the apostle Paul's teaching of redemption through the blood of Jesus.

THE BLOOD OF BULLS

French theologian Alfred Loisy, who died in 1940, believed that a Mithraic rite involving bulls' blood was the basis for the Christian belief that people are saved "through the blood" of Jesus. He specifically linked this ritual to Paul's imagery in Romans 6, where the apostle talks about "all of us who were baptized into Christ Jesus were baptized into his death."[91]

I asked Yamauchi to describe the rite.

"This rite was practiced by Mithraists only in exceptional

cases," he said. "In its developed form, the person was placed in a pit, and a bull was slaughtered on a grate above him, drenching him in the bull's blood.

"This rite is reported in the second century AD," Yamauchi continued, "so there's no way this rite could have influenced Christianity's theology about redemption."

One by one, the grandiose claims that Christianity copied itself after Mithraism had been convincingly swept away by solid scholarship. It was staggering to me that writers could so irresponsibly—or maliciously—make claims about parallels that simply aren't accurate.

"Do you see any evidence that Christianity borrowed *any* of its beliefs from Mithraism?" I asked Yamauchi.

"Not really," he said. "They were rivals in the second century and later. But there's no evidence of Mithraism influencing first-century Christianity. Far from copying Mithraism, the church leaders—from Justin Martyr to Tertullian—denounced Mithraism as a satanic imitation. Some scholars have suggested Christianity may have consciously or unconsciously borrowed minor practices much later, which could be true. This has no impact on Christianity's foundational beliefs, however," Yamauchi concluded.

Along those lines, E. J. Yarnold of Oxford University suggests Mithraism may have influenced a fourth-century Christian practice of having converts renounce Satan in a special ceremony that's no longer practiced. But Yarnold warned against reading too much into the scant remnants of Mithraism. "The modern Mithraic scholar," he said, "is often seduced by apparent lack of evidence to grasp at straws which offer little or no support to his argument."[92]

THE USUAL SUSPECTS

I turned our conversation to the issue of whether any other gods in antiquity might have provided the prototype for the resurrection stories about Jesus. Essentially, I wanted to see whether Yamauchi would agree with what Licona had told me about the matter.

Yamauchi went down the list of the "usual suspects" who appear in popular literature: Marduk, Dionysus, Tammuz, Adonis, Attis, and Osiris.

The contrast with Jesus, said Yamauchi, couldn't be more stark. "All of these myths are repetitive, symbolic representations of the death and rebirth of vegetation. These are not historical figures, and none of their deaths were intended to provide salvation," he pointed out. "In the case of Jesus, even non-Christian authorities, like Josephus and Tacitus, report that he died under Pontius Pilate in the reign of Tiberius. The reports of his resurrection are quite early and are rooted in eyewitness accounts.

"They have the ring of reality," he stressed, "not the ethereal qualities of myth."

CLAIMS OF OTHER VIRGIN BIRTHS

Matthew, a follower of Jesus, and Luke, a first-century physician who said he "carefully investigated everything" about Jesus "from the beginning,"[93] both report that Jesus was born to a virgin. It's an extraordinarily improbable claim—*unless* the resurrection of Jesus is true, in which case his divinity was convincingly established and a virgin birth becomes much more believable.

One of the most popular objections to Jesus, however, is

that his virgin birth was not historical, but was stolen from earlier mythology. "The notion that Jesus had no human father because he was the Son of God...was originally a pagan notion," said Robert J. Miller, associate professor of religion at Juniata College.[94]

I asked Yamauchi for his assessment. "The idea of the virgin birth of Jesus is distinctive because it's based on ancient prophecy, specifically the translation of Isaiah 7:14 into Greek, in the translation of the Old Testament called the Septuagint," he began in response. "As you know, Isaiah uses the Hebrew word *almah*, which means a 'young woman' would give birth, and the Septuagint makes her virginity more explicit by using the Greek word *parthenos*, which specifically means 'virgin.' Of course, it should be said that a young maiden in those days was assumed to be a virgin; we can't necessarily say that in our contemporary society."[95]

"What about the parallels that are often cited between Jesus' virgin birth and mythological gods?" I asked.

"Some of these supposed parallels break down upon close examination," he said. "Some of those that are often cited—like Zeus, for example—are gods who lust after human women, which is decidedly different from Jesus' story. The mythological offspring are half gods and half men, and their lives begin at conception, as opposed to Jesus, who is fully God and fully man and who is also eternal but came into this world through the incarnation. Also, the Gospels put Jesus in a historical context, unlike the mythological gods. On top of that, even if a story of an extraordinary birth in mythology predates Christianity, that doesn't mean Christians appropriated it."

That last point is also made by Robert Gromacki, a professor at Cedarville University, in his 2002 book *The Virgin Birth*:

This is a perfect example of the logical fallacy *post hoc ergo propter hoc* ("after this, therefore, because of this"). Plato wrote about the existence of God long before Paul authored his epistles, but the latter was in no way dependent upon the Greek philosopher. The argument of pagan derivation assumes too much in the way of parallelism and overlooks the radical differences.[96]

I pulled out a list of the most commonly mentioned parallels to the Jesus account. "What about Dionysus—the god of wine and fertility who's also known as Bacchus?" I asked. "He's frequently cited as being the product of a virgin birth."

"No, there's no evidence of a virgin birth for Dionysus," Yamauchi said. "As the story goes, Zeus, disguised as a human, fell in love with the princess Semelê (the daughter of Cadmus), and she became pregnant. Hera, who was Zeus' queen, arranged to have Semelê burned to a crisp, but Zeus rescued the fetus [Dionysus] and sewed him into his thigh until Dionysus was born. So this is not a virgin birth in any sense."[97]

"What about the story of Zeus impregnating Danaë through a shower of gold and her giving birth to Perseus?" I asked.

"There are many stories about Zeus and his liaisons with human women. Here's the big difference: The Jewish God—Yahweh—could be anthropomorphic, but these metaphors were not to be taken literally; whereas in Greek mythology, the anthropomorphism was taken quite literally. The gods were very human—they lusted after mortal women. That's the focus of these myths. Although Yahweh is sometimes expressed in human imagery, he is utterly unlike human beings. So these parallels break down on a very fundamental level. You're talking about two very different concepts of God."[98]

Claims about the extraordinary births of mythological gods were one thing, but allegations that certain pre-Christian *historical* figures—from Buddha to Alexander the Great—are the products of virgin births are something else altogether. I planned to pursue these parallels next.

OTHER REPORTS FROM HISTORY

My first question involved the conception of Alexander the Great. Several stories swirl around his birth.

"There's no question that Alexander's mother was Olympias and his father was Philip of Macedon," Yamauchi explained. "It was only as Philip's son that Alexander inherited the throne when his father was assassinated in 336 BC. The story about Olympias being impregnated by Zeus [while she slept] was propaganda designed to support Alexander's demand for worship."

Indeed, there's a report by Plutarch that Olympias explicitly rejected the story of Alexander's conception by Zeus, saying in reference to Zeus' wife, "Will not Alexander cease slandering me to Hera?"[99] "Actually," said historian Peter Green, "the truth of the matter is that we have surprisingly little direct evidence about Alexander's childhood from any source, and what does exist is of very limited historical value."[100]

Yamauchi continued. "Buddha's birth is often called virginal, but that's not accurate, either," he said. "Sources for the life of Buddha do not appear in written form until five centuries after his death, so they're not very reliable historically. According to legend, Buddha's mother dreamed that he entered her in the form of a white elephant—fully formed! In addition, she had been married for many years prior to this, so she certainly wasn't a virgin.[101]

"The later sources for Buddha, coming 500 to 1,500 years after his life, exaggerate the supernatural elements of his life. It's even possible that some of the supposed parallels to the life of Jesus may have been borrowed from Christianity."[102]

As an aside, Yamauchi's reference to Buddha reminded me of a figure tied to another Eastern religion. "Some authors mention the Hindu god Krishna as having been born of a virgin," I said.

Yamauchi quickly dispatched that claim. "That's not accurate," he replied. "Krishna was born to a mother who already had seven previous sons, as even his followers readily concede."[103]

"What about Zoroaster?"

"Zoroaster lived before 1000 BC, according to Mary Boyce, or in the sixth century BC, according to other scholars," Yamauchi said. "The idea that his mother conceived him by drinking a drink appears in the ninth century AD. That's an extremely long time later—and far after Jesus."

"What's your opinion, then, of this allegation that the virgin birth of Jesus was copied from these other stories?"

"No, there are too many differences," he said. "I don't think anyone can make a convincing case that the virgin birth of Jesus—which was reported quite soon after the fact and in documents that are sober in their reporting—was derived from any pagan or other sources."

In the end, allegations about Christianity stealing its belief about the virgin birth fared no better than the claims that it copied Jesus' resurrection from dying and rising gods in antiquity. In the words of the University of Chicago's renowned historian of religion, Mircea Eliade: "There is no reason to suppose that primitive Christianity was influenced by the Hellenistic mysteries."[104]

Efficiently and authoritatively, Yamauchi had dismantled the plagiarism case that has been hyped by so many critics of Christianity. I decided to wrap up my interview by asking about ways unsuspecting readers can protect themselves from fiction masquerading as fact.

WILL TRUTH WIN OUT?

"Do you think that in this age of the Internet, where half-truths and misinformation keep getting recycled, scholars are doomed to forever be responding to overblown claims that were answered years ago?" I asked.

"Yes, unfortunately, probably so," Yamauchi said, his tone resigned.

"Do you think in the end the truth will win out?"

"For some people," he answered. "For others—they're looking for what they want to find."

I wanted some guidance for those interested in pursuing the truth. "What advice would you give to people looking for reliable information?"

Yamauchi put down his cup of coffee. "First, be careful of articles on the Web. Even though the Internet is a quick and convenient source of information, it also perpetuates outdated and disproved theories," he said. "Also check the credentials of the authors. Do they have the training and depth of knowledge to write authoritatively on these issues? And be sure to check the dates of sources that are quoted. Are they relying on unhistorical claims or discredited scholars? And finally, be aware of the biases of many modern authors, who may clearly have an axe to grind."

Two millennia ago, the apostle Peter was equally unambiguous: The accounts about Jesus in the pages of the New Testament weren't distilled from imaginative stories about mythological deities. Peter wasn't reporting rumors or speculation, and he certainly wasn't trusting his future to the likes of Zeus or Osiris. He was only interested in the *real* Jesus.

"We did not follow cleverly invented stories when we told you about the power and coming of our Lord Jesus Christ," he declared, "but we were eyewitnesses of his majesty."[105]

Jesus Was an Impostor Who Failed to Fulfill the Prophecies about the Messiah

"The response has been volcanic."

David Brickner, the executive director of Jews for Jesus, is soft-spoken and mild-mannered—and if anything, his assessment of what occurred in New York City during the summer of 2006 might actually be an understatement.

In a month-long evangelistic campaign, Brickner led 200 missionaries through all five boroughs of the city, which has the largest Jewish population outside of Israel. They mailed 80,000 Yiddish copies of the *Jesus* film to Jewish homes, distributed a million tracts, and plastered advertisements in subway stations and newspapers.

"We're saying Jesus is the Messiah of Israel," said Brickner. "What could be more Jewish?"[106]

For many, the reaction was emotional—to say the least. "Jews for Jesus Hit Town and Find a Tough Crowd," said a headline in the *New York Times*.[107] Though much of the response came in the form of quiet indignation, one incensed commuter did punch an evangelist in the mouth, and copies of the Jesus film were publicly burned.[108]

A "counter-missionary" organization called Jews for Judaism stationed its own volunteers close to Brickner's evangelists and even staffed a toll-free hotline for family members wanting to bring back a relative who decided to follow Jesus.

"Someone is trying to get you to betray not just your religion, but your parents and your grandparents," warned David Berger, professor of religion at Brooklyn College.[109] In his own understatement, Rabbi Joshua Waxman wrote: "Jews for Jesus push a lot of people's buttons." For him, the issues are straightforward: "Couldn't you be Jewish and believe in Jesus? The answer is no."[110]

One conviction that unites many Jewish and Christian scholars is that the *Tanakh*, known by Christians as the Old Testament, does foretell the coming of the Messiah. "Belief in the coming of the Messiah has always been a fundamental part of Judaism," said Rabbi Aryeh Kaplan. "It is a concept that is repeated again and again throughout the length and breadth of Jewish literature."[111]

The big controversy is whether Jesus of Nazareth is the one who fulfilled the ancient prophecies and thus fits the fingerprint of this much-anticipated Messiah, a word that means "anointed one." The Greek word for Messiah is *christos*, or Christ, the term that has been firmly affixed to Jesus' name throughout history.

If these predictions really did come true in Jesus of Nazareth, the implications are enormous for everyone, not just those with a Jewish background. First, this would confirm the supernatural nature of the Bible, since the odds of anyone fulfilling so many ancient prophecies—by one estimate, 127 personal messianic predictions in 3,348 verses of the Old Testament[112]—by mere chance would be mathematically prohibitive.

Second, if Jesus—and only Jesus—fulfilled these ancient

forecasts, then this would be a definitive affirmation of his identity as the One sent by God to be the Savior of Israel and the world. Of course, the reverse is equally significant. Jesus said in Luke 24:44: "Everything must be fulfilled that is written about me in the Law of Moses, the Prophets and the Psalms." When a Samaritan woman said to him, "I know that Messiah" (called Christ) "is coming," Jesus replied: "I who speak to you am he."[113] Having made these unambiguous claims, if he then fails to match the prophetic portrait, Jesus would be an impostor worthy of rejection and disdain—a false prophet who should be rejected by Jews and Gentiles alike.

Could Jesus really have been the Christ? What happens when emotions subside and the evidence is systematically examined? How strong is the case for Jesus the Messiah—and can it withstand the most potent objections of those who deny that he was described in prophecies dating back hundreds of years before his birth in Bethlehem?

Those are the issues that prompted me to fly to North Carolina and to seek out one of the world's leading authorities on the messianic prophecies.

INTERVIEW #5: MICHAEL L. BROWN, PHD

As a teenager growing up on Long Island, Michael Brown's insatiable appetite for illicit drugs earned him the nicknames "Iron Man" and "Drug Bear." By the age of 15, the aspiring rock-and-roll drummer was shooting heroin and burglarizing homes and even a doctor's office for amusement—an incongruous lifestyle for the son of the senior lawyer of the New York Supreme Court.

He grew up in a Jewish family, but he was uninterested in spiritual matters. When Brown was bar mitzvahed at the age of

13, he was given a Hebrew passage to memorize—but nobody ever translated it for him, and he never bothered to ask anyone what the words meant. For him, it was a meaningless ritual.

> **Bar Mitzvah**
>
> A Jewish ceremony for celebrating the coming of age; for boys, it's held at age 13; for girls, it (called bat mitzvah) takes place when they are 12.

In 1971 the two other members of Brown's band began attending a local church because they were in pursuit of two girls who were related to the pastor. But little by little, the gospel began to influence them. Upset by the changes in their lives, Brown decided to visit the church in an effort to extricate them. One of the girls, aware of his reputation, wrote in her diary that night: "Anti-Christ comes to church."

Bio: Michael Brown

- Doctorate in Near Eastern Languages and Literatures from New York University
- Taught at Trinity Evangelical Divinity School, Fuller Theological Seminary, and Regent University, and in 25 countries
- Author of 18 books, including the multivolume series *Answering Jewish Objections to Jesus*
- Contributor to *Oxford Dictionary of the Jewish Religion* and *New International Dictionary of Old Testament Theology and Exegesis,* as well as several Semitic linguistic journals

Unexpectedly, in the months that followed, Brown discovered a new emotion: A gnawing sense of regret and conviction over his rebellious and drug-saturated behavior. He ended up in many discussions with Christians about spirituality. Then on November 12, 1971, the pastor asked if anyone wanted to receive Jesus as their Savior, and Brown walked down the aisle—not because he really wanted to become a Christian, but so he could give the congregation a thrill. After all, he was sure they regarded him as the worst of sinners.

Then something even more unexpected happened: As he repeated the words of the pastor in a prayer of repentance and faith, he found himself suddenly believing the message of Christ. "It was like a light went on," he said. Instantly, he believed Jesus had died for his sins and had risen from the dead. "I knew it was real," Brown said. "Now the challenge was: What was I going to do with it—because I wasn't ready to change my lifestyle." It wasn't until five weeks later that he permanently abandoned drugs and yielded his life to Jesus.

His father liked the improvement in Brown's behavior, but he didn't like the Jesus part. He took his son to talk to the local rabbi, who eventually took him to a community of ultra-Orthodox Jews in Brooklyn. None of them, however, was able to dislodge his belief, now confirmed by his own deep study, that Jesus is the Messiah of Israel.

Branches of Judaism

Within Judaism are several branches, just as within Protestant Christianity there are many denominations. The main branches of Judaism are Orthodox, Conservative, and Reform. Some people also include Reconstructionist and Humanistic Judaism. You can find a brief description of these different branches at http://judaism.about.com/.

But they did raise some serious questions, challenging him on his lack of a working knowledge of Hebrew. To better understand and test the messianic promises, Brown then pursued years of education that ultimately led to a master's degree, as well as a doctorate, in Near Eastern Languages and Literatures from New York University. His practice of tackling the most powerful arguments of critics has helped him develop into one of America's best-known defenders of Jesus the Messiah. Over the past 30 years, he's debated and dialogued with rabbis and leaders of the Jewish community on radio, television, and college campuses, and even in synagogues.

Before my visit, I'd reviewed the most current objections to Jesus being the Messiah—an easy task, since I'd already overseen two debates on the topic. Frankly, I thought some of the arguments against Jesus' fulfillment of the prophecies were weak, their answers so obvious that they weren't worth bringing up. But I had to admit there were many others that raised significant and thorny issues. I wrote those down and then added the questions that had been troubling me personally.

On a brisk morning, with the sun shining through fiery autumn leaves, I found Brown's office in a nondescript white building in a northern suburb of Charlotte.

THE *SHEKINAH* AND THE *MEMRA*

"Let's be really honest," I began. "The prophecies don't foretell that the Messiah would be divine, do they?"

Brown leaned forward. "Actually, Lee, yes, they do," he replied.

I glanced down at my clipboard. "Not according to the late Orthodox rabbi Aryeh Kaplan," I told him. "'In no place do the Prophets say that he will be anything more than a remarkable leader and teacher,' he said. 'The Jewish Messiah is truly human in origin. He is born of ordinary human parents, and is of flesh and blood like all mortals.'"[114]

Moving to the edge of his chair, Brown said, "Let's look at the facts. There are definitely verses that point toward his divine nature. Bear in mind, however, that the Jews were staunch monotheists. They believed that there is only one God, and they wouldn't have understood prophecies about a Messiah who is God."

"So what's the evidence for his predicted divinity?" I asked.

"The Messiah is described as a king in the line of King David who will be highly exalted and will someday rule and reign. The Hebrew Scriptures use several parallel descriptions to describe both God and this exalted king: People will praise God, and the people will praise the king; people will serve God, and the people will serve the king; people will bow down before God, and the people will bow down before the king.

"The Messiah as described in Daniel 7 [verse 13]—the Son of Man—is highly exalted; he comes before the throne of God, he is worshiped, he is given sovereign power and authority, and his kingdom is eternal. Being worshiped, having sovereignty, being eternal—those sound a lot like divine characteristics to me. And of course, Jesus' favorite self-description was the Son of Man, and he applied Daniel 7 directly to himself.[115]

"Even more explicitly, Psalm 45 says of the Messiah-king, 'Your throne, O God, will last for ever and ever.' God is anointing this king, yet the king himself is called *Elohim*, a Hebrew name for God. That's very significant. We know that sometimes *Elohim* can be a reference to earthly judges and angels, but to call an individual *Elohim* in this context is really stretching things.

"Isaiah 52:13 says the servant will be 'high' and 'lifted up.'[116] In Isaiah, those words only occur in reference to the Lord. And even more directly, in Isaiah 9:6-7, the king is given various names, including 'Mighty God' and 'Everlasting Father.' So you have that royal king, the Messiah, being described as divine."

"Did the people of that day anticipate a divine Messiah?"

"It wasn't really until Yeshua came that they looked back at the Hebrew Scriptures and said, 'Oh, *that* explains it!' In hindsight, it becomes much clearer."

> **Yeshua**
>
> The Jewish name for Jesus

"But the Hebrew Scriptures say *God is one* and doesn't have a body," I protested.[117] "The Bible says nobody can ever see God.[118] So how could Jesus be God?"

"It's clear there's only one God, yet it seems that he's somehow complex in his unity," Brown explained. "On the one hand, he's ruling from his throne in heaven; and yet on the other hand, he's present on the earth. There are other times when he is seen, even though the Bible says no one can see God, who is spirit. Let me give you a few examples. In Genesis 18, Yahweh and two angels appear to Abraham. Jacob saw God face to face.[119] Isaiah says, 'I saw the Lord.'[120] Exodus 24:9-10 says, 'Moses and Aaron, Nadab and Abihu, and the seventy elders of Israel went up and saw the God of Israel.'"

I jumped in. "Wasn't that just a *vision*?"

"No, because verse 11 says, 'God did not raise his hand against these leaders of the Israelites.' That doesn't sound like a vision to me," Brown said, a chuckle in his voice. "So who is it that all these people saw if they can't see God, and yet they saw God? Could it have been the Son?"

Without waiting for a response, he said, "Yes, I believe it

was. Then the New Testament begins to enlighten us—God is complex in his unity, and this one God makes himself known as the Father, Son, and Spirit. The Father has never been seen; the Son is the one who reveals [the Father] and makes him known and who now takes on flesh and blood. So in a sense, God did not become a mere man, which agrees with what the Hebrew Scriptures emphatically say. But can [God] make himself known in flesh and blood? Can he, while remaining enthroned in heaven, come down among us?

Shekinah

The English spelling of a Hebrew word for the visible presence of God. The word *Shekinah* itself is not found in Scripture, but Jewish and Christian scholars identify times when God revealed himself through the *Shekinah*: when, in the pillar of cloud, he led the people of Israel out of Egypt, when he appeared to Moses in the burning bush and on Mount Sinai, and when God's glory filled the Holy of Holies in the temple.

"This explains how all of these things can be said at the same time about God. Interestingly, the rabbis came up with different concepts about how God can be untouchable and invisible, yet touchable and known. One of the concepts was the *Shekinah*, which is the living presence of God on Earth. God said in Exodus 25:8, 'Have them make a sanctuary for me, and I will dwell among them.' One rabbi said to me, 'So Jesus was like a walking *Shekinah*—that's what you believe?' I said, '*Exactly*.'

"We also see references in the Hebrew Scriptures to the Word of God. The Word is something that proceeds forth from him, yet *is* him. We see in Genesis that God created all things through his spoken word—in fact, Psalm 33:6 says, 'By the word of the Lord were the heavens made.' His Word is even worthy of praise. Psalm 56:4 says, 'In God, whose word I praise, in God I trust.' The *Targums*, which are Aramaic paraphrases of the Hebrew Scriptures, use the expression *Memra*, which is 'Word.' For instance, instead of saying "The Lord spoke to Moses," it says "The Word of the Lord spoke to Moses."

> **Memra**
>
> Aramaic for "word," used when referring to the Word of God

"So now go to John 1:1, 14 and merely substitute Memra for 'Word': 'In the beginning was the *Memra*, and the *Memra* was with God, and the *Memra* was God...The *Memra* became flesh and made his dwelling among us.' This is God drawing near. He was in the tabernacle; now he's in Yeshua, who combines deity and humanity. Though he remains God, he reveals himself fully in bodily form.

"If John had simply written, '*God* became a human being,' it would have given the false impression that the Lord was no longer filling the universe or reigning in heaven, but that he had abandoned his throne to take up residence here, like one of the pagan deities. Instead, John tells us that it was the divine *Word* that became a human being, and through the Word, we can know God personally. As John said, 'No one has ever seen God; the only Son, who is in the bosom of the Father, he has made him known.'[121]

"Seeing Jesus was seeing God. Jesus said in John 14:9, 'Anyone who has seen me has seen the Father.' He also said, 'I and the Father are one.'[122] Notice that Jesus didn't call himself 'God';

he called himself 'God's Son'[123] —the one in whom the fullness of God dwells in bodily form.[124]

"This doesn't contradict anything in the Hebrew Scriptures," he said in conclusion. "In fact, this explains many verses in the Hebrew Bible that are otherwise unintelligible."

WHERE IS WORLD PEACE?

Nevertheless, I knew that one of the biggest objections brought up by the critics is the fact that Jesus didn't fulfill what they consider to be the main messianic prophecies: Bringing about a world of peace and unity and ending evil, idolatry, falsehood, and hatred.

Kaplan was especially blunt. "What can a Jew lose by embracing Christianity?" he asked. "The answer is *everything*." He added,

> The Jews had one major objection to the Christian Messiah, and that was the fact that he had been unsuccessful. Judaism had always taught that the Messiah would redeem Israel in a political sense, and Jesus had failed to accomplish this. Instead, he had been scourged and humiliated like a common rebel, and finally crucified along with two ordinary thieves. How could the career of Jesus be reconciled with the glorious picture of the Messiah as taught by the Prophets of Israel? The early Christians faced this dilemma, and, in justifying Jesus as the Messiah, radically altered the entire concept.[125]

Amy-Jill Levine, a Jewish expert on Jesus and the New Testament at Vanderbilt Divinity School and author of *The Misunder-*

stood Jew, said Jesus cannot be the Messiah because he didn't accomplish what was prophesied that the Messiah would do. "The Messiah is someone who establishes justice throughout the world. And I look out my window and I know that hasn't happened," she said.[126]

Christians, of course, offer a radically different perspective. "Not all of the prophecies in the Old Testament about the Messiah were fulfilled in Jesus' lifetime," historian Edwin Yamauchi said in a TV documentary called Who Is This Jesus: Is He Risen? "The Christians' answer to that is that those prophecies will be fulfilled when Christ comes again a second time in glory."[127]

Comes again? Jewish scholars point out that the terms "first coming" and "second coming" aren't even mentioned in the Old Testament. They contend that Christians invented the idea of Jesus coming again out of their embarrassment that he failed to usher in the universal peace the Messiah is predicted to bring.

"In light of that," I said after mentioning this to Brown, "how can you say Jesus is the Messiah?"

"Yeshua fulfilled the essential prophecies that had a definite time frame and which had to be completed before the second temple was destroyed [in AD 70]," Brown said.[128] "This is not a matter of speculation; it's historical fact. And since he fulfilled the past prophecies—coming as our great high priest and making atonement for our sins—we can be sure he'll fulfill the future prophecies—reigning as the worldwide king and bringing peace to the earth.

"In fact, he already rules and reigns as royal king over the lives of tens of millions of people from every nation under the sun. They give him their total allegiance and loyalty. And that's only the beginning; he will reign over all when he returns.

"Also," he said, "it's not as if Yeshua did part of the job of the

Messiah and then quit for 2,000 years. Instead, we see certain things unfolding just as expected, with his kingdom continuing to advance. Look at how many people came to worship the one true God in the 20th century alone. This tells me the pace is accelerating. So the fulfillment of the first stage, as well as the ongoing fulfillment of those things that had to be ongoing, tells me that the final stage is clear."

"But the term *second coming* isn't found in the Hebrew Scriptures," I pointed out.

"The word *trinity* isn't used anywhere in the entire Bible either, but the evidence is there supporting it," he countered. "The prophecies require certain events to happen—like atonement and the divine visitation to the temple—before other events can happen, like the Messiah bringing peace to the earth. The first act precedes the second act and prepares the way for it. First, atonement for sin; then peace on the earth. Yeshua did what needed to be done before AD 70. So we can have confidence he'll do what needs to be done in the future."

"Some say Jesus didn't fulfill any of the *provable* prophecies," I said. "Anyone could die, anyone could claim to have been born in Bethlehem as Micah 5:2 foretold, and so forth."

"One simple response: The story of his deliverance from death, according to Psalm 22, was supposed to have such an effect that people around the world turned to God," Brown said. "That's pretty provable. Rejected by your own people but being a light to the nations—that's pretty provable. There's the ongoing accreditation by God of who he is, through the extension of his kingdom around the world. It's convincing enough to read the amazing accounts of Yeshua in the New Testament. It's quite another to see how he continues, without a break, to have worldwide impact."

REPENTANCE AND SACRIFICE

Critics have also attacked Christianity's claim that Jesus' atoning death is the culmination of the Old Testament practice of animal sacrifices. I pulled out a document from Jews for Judaism and read it to Brown:

> None of the biblical prophets taught that animal or blood sacrifices were indispensable in order for the forgiveness of our sins. As a matter of fact, the prophets constantly berated people who mistakenly thought that sacrifices, in and of themselves, bring about forgiveness. The Bible clearly teaches that the only way of atoning for sins is through repentance—a process of transformation that includes acknowledging our wrongdoing and confessing it to G-d, feeling regret, making restitution if we harmed someone, resolving to improve our behavior, returning to G-d and praying for forgiveness."[129]

The Name of G-d

By tradition, many religious Jews don't spell out God's name as a sign of respect and to prevent the name from being defaced. Instead, they use "G-d."

I slipped the Jews for Judaism paper back into my briefcase and looked at Brown. "If repentance is all that's needed," I said, "doesn't that negate the belief that Jesus was the fulfillment of the Jewish sacrificial system?"

"Let's make something clear," Brown began. "The new covenant writings—that is, the writings of the New Testament—

consistently emphasize the importance of repentance as well. They don't teach that Jesus died and therefore you're automatically forgiven. Jesus said, 'Repent, for the kingdom of heaven is near.'[130] He said, 'I have not come to call the righteous, but sinners to repentance.'[131] In Mark 6, he sends out the Twelve—and what do they preach? That people should repent.[132]

"I don't argue that," he went on. "But repentance has never existed independently from the larger system of atonement that God made. God was trying to get something across, which was the foundational nature of the blood sacrifice. That system was pointing toward the One who would come. God never really wanted the blood of bulls and goats. The prophets rejected sacrifices that were offered with an empty heart; they never rejected sacrifices themselves..."

I cut in. "But doesn't God say in Hosea 6:6, 'For I desire mercy, *not sacrifice,* and acknowledgment of God rather than burnt offerings'?"[133]

"Jesus quoted that *twice* in the New Testament. I agree with that!" he declared. "The problem was *not* the sacrifice; it was the empty heart. In 1 Samuel 15, we read that God prefers obedience to sacrifice. What he wants is an obedient heart.[134] Yet because we all fall short, he established the sacrificial system to ultimately point people toward the Messiah.

"You needed repentance and you needed the blood. That's the whole message of the new covenant to Jew and Gentile alike: Turn in repentance toward God and put your trust in Jesus' atoning sacrifice. He's the 'Lamb of God who takes away the sin of the world.'"

Though Brown had answered my basic questions about the atonement system, one last issue was left hanging. "Sacrificing animals seems like such a barbaric practice," I said. "These days the animal-rights folks would howl in protest."

"In the culture of the day, it was perfectly normal to offer sacrifices as part of worship," came his response. "It was saying, 'I'm taking something valuable that I have and offering it up to God.' But ultimately, God was not interested in that. He was interested in something of massive eternal value, which is showing us how ugly sin is and how he was going to send a substitute. So for centuries and centuries—because it takes people a while to get the point—he kept giving the same lesson, until he finally sent the One who brought an end to the necessity of blood sacrifices."

THE SUFFERING SERVANT

A significant part of Brown's case for Jesus being the Messiah hinges on the prophecies of Isaiah. Of special interest is the description of the suffering servant in Isaiah 52:13 to 53:12, which has probably prompted more people to put their trust in Jesus as the Messiah than any other passage in Scripture:[135]

See, my servant will act wisely;

   he will be raised and lifted up and highly exalted.

Just as there were many who were appalled at him—

   his appearance was so disfigured beyond that of any man

   and his form marred beyond human likeness—

so will he sprinkle many nations,

   and kings will shut their mouths because of him.

For what they were not told, they will see,

   and what they have not heard, they will understand.

Who has believed our message
  and to whom has the arm of the LORD been revealed?
He grew up before him like a tender shoot,
  and like a root out of dry ground.
He had no beauty or majesty to attract us to him,
  nothing in his appearance that we should desire him.
He was despised and rejected by men,
  a man of sorrows, and familiar with suffering.
Like one from whom men hide their faces
  he was despised, and we esteemed him not.

Surely he took up our infirmities
  and carried our sorrows,
yet we considered him stricken by God,
  smitten by him, and afflicted.
But he was pierced for our transgressions,
  he was crushed for our iniquities;
the punishment that brought us peace was upon him,
  and by his wounds we are healed.
We all, like sheep, have gone astray,
  each of us has turned to his own way;
and the LORD has laid on him
  the iniquity of us all.

He was oppressed and afflicted,
  yet he did not open his mouth;
he was led like a lamb to the slaughter,

and as a sheep before her shearers is silent,
    so he did not open his mouth.
By oppression and judgment he was taken away.
    And who can speak of his descendants?
For he was cut off from the land of the living;
    for the transgression of my people he was stricken.
He was assigned a grave with the wicked,
    and with the rich in his death,
Though he had done no violence,
    nor was any deceit in his mouth.

Yet it was the LORD's will to crush him and cause him to suffer,
    and though the Lord makes his life a guilt offering,
he will see his offspring and prolong his days,
    and the will of the LORD will prosper in his hand.
After the suffering of his soul,
    he will see the light of life and be satisfied;
by his knowledge my righteous servant will justify many,
    and he will bear their iniquities.
Therefore I will give him a portion among the great,
    and he will divide the spoils with the strong,
because he poured out his life unto death,
    and was numbered with the transgressors.
For he bore the sin of many,
    and made intercession for the transgressors.

"It's almost as if God said, 'I want to make it so absolutely clear that Yeshua is the Messiah that it's undeniable,'" Brown declared.

I decided to raise some of the most frequent objections to its fulfillment in Jesus and see how Brown would respond.

OBJECTIONS TO ISAIAH

Some commentators, I pointed out, say this description of the suffering servant applies to the people of Israel as a nation, not to an individual who is the Messiah. "Doesn't the passage actually deal with the return of the Jewish people from the Babylonian exile, which occurred more than 500 years before Jesus was born?" I asked.

"That's the backdrop of many of the messianic prophecies," Brown said, "but nowhere in the classical, foundational, authoritative Jewish writings do we find the interpretation that this passage refers to the nation of Israel. References to the servant as a people actually end with Isaiah 48:20.

"Many traditional Jewish interpreters, from the *Targum* to today, had no problem seeing this passage as referring to the Messiah," he went on. "By the sixteenth century, Rabbi Moshe Alshech said, 'Our rabbis with one voice accept and affirm the opinion that the prophet is speaking of the Messiah, and we shall ourselves also adhere to the same view.' So he was saying all his contemporaries agreed with the messianic reading— even though it must have been very tempting to deny this, because by that time Christians had been claiming for centuries that this passage describes Yeshua."

Targum

An Aramaic translation of the Hebrew Bible

"Why can't this passage refer to Israel as a whole?"

"Several reasons," he said. "The servant of the Lord is righteous and without guile and yet suffers terribly. That doesn't describe Israel at that time; the book of Isaiah actually starts with the Lord describing Israel as a "sinful nation, a people loaded with guilt, a brood of evildoers."[136]

"But in another chapter," I said, "the psalmist says Israel suffered at the hands of its enemies even though it was righteous."[137]

"Not so," he responded. "This is a prayer of the righteous remnant on behalf of the sinning nation. It's the small group of the godly—the righteous—who are interceding on behalf of the unrighteous, ungodly, suffering majority."

"Okay," I said, conceding the point. "I interrupted you—you said there were several reasons why this passage doesn't refer to the nation of Israel."

"Yes, the second reason is because the text says the servant will be highly exalted, even to where kings stand in awe. That's not true of Israel, but it is true of Yeshua, who's worshiped by kings and leaders around the world. And third, Isaiah says the servant's sufferings brought healing to the people. Now, has Israel suffered through the ages? Yes, but our sufferings did not bring healing to the nations that afflicted us."

"All right, this passage might refer to an individual—but it can't be Yeshua," I said.

"Why not?"

"Let me give you several reasons." I consulted the series of objections I'd jotted down. "First, the Isaiah passage says nobody was attracted to the servant of the Lord, but we know Jesus attracted huge throngs to himself—thousands of people flocked to him at times."

"Actually, Isaiah 53 first refers to his origins, which were very lowly and inauspicious—'He grew up before him like a tender shoot, and like a root out of dry ground.'[138] That's a consistent theme in the New Testament—'Can anything good come out of Nazareth? The carpenter's son? *Him*? How could this be?'"[139] said Brown.

"Isaiah 53:2 says, 'He had no beauty or majesty to attract us to him,' and certainly there's nothing recorded about the appearance of Jesus that would contradict that. Besides, the crowds around Jesus were very fickle—they shouted, 'Crown him!' one day and "Crucify him!' the next. But the primary thrust of Isaiah 53 is his rejection, suffering, and death—at that time, he's utterly forsaken. Yeshua fulfills all of that very well."

"His death?" I said. "Critics claim that the passage doesn't specifically and unambiguously say the servant would die."

"There's an accumulation of words that are used," Brown said. "He's stricken by God, he's smitten, he's pierced, he's crushed, he's oppressed, he's afflicted, he's led like a lamb to the slaughter, he's taken away, he's cut off from the land of the living, he's assigned a grave, he poured out his life unto death, he's with the rich in his death—what are all those phrases referring to, if not the fact that he did truly die?"

"But what about the resurrection?" I pressed. "Show me where that word is used."

"It's not—but it's plainly implied," replied Brown. "How does someone die and yet 'prolong his days'? Clearly, the passage speaks of the servant's continued activities after his death. And there's only one explanation for that—resurrection!"

WHO BUT JESUS?

Brown's answers seemed persuasive enough, but there were still other reasons why critics reject Isaiah 53's fulfillment in Jesus. For instance, while the Isaiah passage refers to the nonviolence of God's servant, the Gospels describe Jesus as using a whip to drive the money changers out of the temple.

"That sounds like a violent act that would get a person arrested today," I said. "Wouldn't that disqualify Jesus from being the Messiah?"

"When the Hebrew Scriptures speak of violence, which in Hebrew is *hamas*, it's describing illegal aggression like murder, bloodshed, and robbery—none of which Yeshua ever committed," Brown said. "Jesus' nonviolence was so well known that Mahatma Gandhi and Martin Luther King, Jr. modeled their nonviolent resistance after him. When Peter drew a sword and cut off the ear of one of the guards who came to arrest Jesus, Jesus rebuked him—and then healed the guard's ear."

While that was true, it seemed to me he was skirting the question. "Specifically, what about the temple cleansing?" I asked.

"As for the temple incident, this was praiseworthy and motivated by zeal for God," Brown replied. "If he wanted to hurt someone, then he would have used a sword; but instead, he made a whip out of cords, which was apparently used for the animals. The money changers got only a verbal rebuke for making the temple 'a den of robbers.'[140] There's no record of anyone being injured, and this incident wasn't even brought up at Jesus' trial, where nobody could accuse him of wrongdoing."

I raised yet another issue. "Isaiah 53 says the Lord's servant will not lift up his voice or cry out, yet Jesus cried out several times on the cross," I said.

"Again, let's look at the context," Brown said. "The passage says 'he did not open his mouth; he was led like a lamb to the slaughter.' Interestingly, the New Testament specifically applies this text to Jesus.[141] All through his ordeal—his arrest, his trial, his flogging, his crucifixion—he doesn't try to defend himself, he doesn't protest, he doesn't fight: Just like a lamb being led to the slaughter. He truly turns the other cheek, as he taught in the Sermon on the Mount.[142] Is he crying out when he says on the cross, 'Father, into your hands I commit my spirit'? Is he crying out when he says, 'Father, forgive them'? Or is that also being like a lamb? The point is, he never fought what was happening to him."

I glanced down at my notes: Only one significant objection remained. "Isaiah 53 says the servant of the Lord will have descendants—or 'see seed' in the Hebrew,"[143] I said. "Jesus never married or had children, so he can't be the Messiah, can he?"

"Can *seed* be used metaphorically, in terms of spiritual offspring?" he asked. "Isaiah uses it that way in other chapters; for example, he calls Israel 'a seed of evildoers.'[144] If we follow a standard Hebrew lexicon, we see that 'seed of evildoers' would mean 'a community of evildoers'[145] or 'evildoers to the core.' In the context of Isaiah 53, *seed* would mean the servant of the Lord would see godly, spiritual posterity, true disciples transformed by means of his labors on their behalf.

"Also, the Hebrew word for *seed* can mean 'a future generation' without reference to specific descendants of one individual in particular. It's used this way in Psalm 22. In the context of Isaiah 53, this would mean the servant of the Lord would see future generations of his people serving the Lord."

"Overall, then, you feel like Isaiah 53 remains the passage with the most clarity—" I began, but Brown interrupted.

"With all due respect to those who come up with objections, they're really swatting at flies," he said. "Any time I can get someone to read this passage, I ask, 'Of whom does this speak?' If you can read it in Hebrew, all the better. You'd be amazed at the reaction. I remember showing it to a respectful Jewish man. He read it, got red in the face, and yelled: 'Jesus Christ!' It was an expression of anger, but I thought, *How ironic is that?*

"Because who but Jesus could it be describing?"[146]

THE RIGHTEOUS SUFFERER

For centuries Christians have cited Psalm 22, the prayer of the righteous sufferer, as foreshadowing the crucifixion of Jesus. It describes the piercing of the hands and feet, the stretching of the body until the "bones are out of joint," the intensity of the thirst, and the dividing of the victim's garments among his persecutors.[147]

Rabbi Tovia Singer has accused Christians of "deliberately mistranslating" this psalm to make it appear as though it points toward Jesus on the cross. He said that while the King James Version renders the Hebrew as, "They pierced my hands and my feet," this is actually "a not-too-ingenious Christian interpolation." The unadulterated Hebrew, he said, should be rendered, "Like a lion, they are at my hands and feet."[148]

"This is a serious allegation," I said to Brown. "Did Christians maliciously tamper with the text?"

"This is definitely not something Christians made up," he said firmly. "The oldest Greek translation—the Septuagint—translated it as, 'they pierced.' The oldest Hebrew copy of the Psalms that we possess, from the Dead Sea Scrolls and dating back to the century before Jesus, uses the Hebrew verb *ka'aru*, which comes from the root meaning 'to bore through'—not *ka'ari*, which means 'like a lion.' The same [is true for] about a dozen medieval manuscripts, which are *the* authoritative texts on traditional Jewish thought. But let me tell you why this really doesn't matter."

"Why?" I asked.

"Let's make the assumption that the correct translation is 'like a lion, they are at my hands and feet.' What is this lion doing with the victim's hands and feet—*licking them?*" His voice was thick with sarcasm.

"A prominent Jewish commentator, Metsudat David, said, 'They crush my hands and my feet as the lion crushes the bones of the prey in its mouth.' So the imagery is clear: The metaphorical lions are tearing and ripping at the sufferer's hands and feet. This mauling and biting graphically portray great physical agony.

"Would this contradict the picture of a crucifixion? In no way. It's entirely consistent with what occurs in a crucifixion. So either translation could be said to foreshadow the suffering of the Messiah. But the bottom line is there's no Christian tampering with the text, just honest efforts to accurately translate the Hebrew [in which] only one character determines the difference between *ka'aru*, or 'pierced,' and *ka'ari*, or 'like a lion.'"

"But how can you consider this psalm to be about the Messiah," I asked, "when it seems to be about David? After all, David wrote it in the first person."

"Many events in David's life were repeated in the life of the Messiah, since David was in many ways the prototype of the Messiah," said Brown. "In fact, a famous rabbinic *midrash*, or commentary, that was written some 1,200 years ago makes the point that David was speaking of the Messiah's sufferings.[149]

"When he was on the cross, Jesus quoted the opening line from Psalm 22—'My God, my God, why have you forsaken me?'" added Brown. "By doing so, he was applying the psalm to himself. The psalm describes the righteous sufferer, publicly mocked and shamed, brought down to the jaws of death in the midst of terrible suffering and humiliation, and miraculously delivered by God, to the praise of his name. So it applies powerfully to Jesus, the ideal righteous sufferer."

"GOD'S VERY BEST"

One more topic begged to be addressed. I had to ask Brown: "Given the depth and breadth of the prophecies—given the compelling portrayal of Jesus in Isaiah 53 alone—why don't more Jewish people come to faith in him?"

Brown had heard the question many times before. "There are several answers," he began. "For the most part, many Jewish people simply don't examine the issue. Religious Jews are engaged in the biblical text, but they don't spend most of their time looking at the prophets; instead, they study the Talmud and rabbinic traditions. They're not looking in the right place to find Yeshua. But many Jews today are not even following God in a devoted way. There's a general lack of God-consciousness. Also, there's a price to pay if a Jewish person decides to follow Jesus: They could be ostracized from their family and community. And another reason, unfortunately, is the barrier put up by anti-Semitism in the past."

That remark stopped me cold. "Do you think Christians are generally oblivious to the history of anti-Semitism and Christianity?" I asked.

"Yes, often they are—for good reason: They haven't seen it, and it isn't in their hearts," he replied. "With almost no exception, the Christians I've met around the world have a special attachment to Jewish people and Israel. So the history of anti-Semitism is very much unknown for that positive reason—but there's also a bad reason."

"Which is?"

"Many Christians today, especially evangelicals, don't have a sense of history. They'll quote Martin Luther left and right, but they won't talk about the horrific things he wrote that Adolph Hitler adopted, like when Luther recommended, among other things, that synagogues be burned, Jewish homes destroyed, and rabbis forbidden to teach under the threat of death.[150] They'll quote the powerful preaching of John Chrysostom, but they won't mention his seven sermons against the Jews, where he said, 'I hate the Jews,' called them 'possessed by the devil,' and said the Jewish religion is 'a disease.'[151]

"Someone once said that those pages of history that Jews have memorized, Christians have torn out of their history books. There's no denying these things occurred, but they were a complete and horrible aberration that, unfortunately, have been used to keep many Jews away from Jesus."

My heart sank at the prospect of anyone being repelled from seeking out the real Jesus because of Christians who, by their repugnant words and attitudes, betrayed Christ's most fundamental teachings.

"What can be done about it?" I asked.

"There was a Scottish Presbyterian conference 150 years ago where they were asking the question, 'To reach out to the Jews, what's the most pressing need?'"

"What was the answer?"

"More tears," Brown said somberly. "And I still believe that remains a pressing issue—more tears. It's essential that as followers of Jesus we repudiate these aberrations of history and tell Jewish people, 'Allow us to show you who Yeshua really is and what he really teaches.'"

"And what about for you personally?" I said. "Who's the real Jesus to you?"

"Yeshua is the right continuation of my Jewish roots," Brown said. "He's the Messiah of Israel and the Savior of the world. He's the One to whom I owe my life, and through him I've come to know God. He is the One who provided me complete forgiveness of sins and who loved me when I was a miserable, ungrateful, rebellious, proud wretch. He put a new heart and a new spirit within me; he has turned my life around and given it meaning. He's the fullness of God in bodily form. He's the very expression and image of the Father—in seeing him, I see and know God.

"And he's the only hope of the world. Outside of him, all we see is darkness. He's the hope of Israel. Israel will run out of options and finally, in the end, recognize that the one who it thought was the source of all its pain and suffering through the years is actually its only hope.

"He's the beginning and the end, the all in all. I cannot imagine existence outside of him. I cannot imagine truth outside of him. I can't imagine purpose in life outside of him. So really, he is the ultimate expression of God to the human race. That's why I'm spending my life talking to Jewish people—as compassionately and accurately as I can—about the reality of Jesus the Messiah.

"I just can't withhold God's very best from those he dearly loves."

People Should Be Free to Pick and Choose What to Believe about Jesus

Wendi was forced to go to Sunday school as a child, but she never believed what she heard. Years later, after suffering a miscarriage, she wanted to know what happened to the unborn baby's soul. "I explored Christianity, but I didn't get any answers that satisfied me," she said in an interview with David Ian Miller for *San Francisco Gate*. So she took a class in metaphysics, where she learned about life after death, intuition, and other intriguing topics.

Now this motivational speaker and life coach has created her own belief system, patching together bits and pieces from Christianity, Buddhism, paganism, metaphysics, and a lot from the Tao-te Ching, which teaches that everything is made of energy. "I take what resonates with me from each religion," she said. Her criterion for picking and choosing elements is based on "what works."

"I believe that everybody's belief system is right for them," she said. "Mine is right for me, yours is right for you, my mom's is right for her, and so on. I don't believe in judging each other the way that I see happening in Christianity and other religions." Rather than trying to convert anyone to her beliefs, she helps others find their own personal god or goddess.[152]

DO-IT-YOURSELF SPIRITUALITY

Increasingly, people seeking religious input draw more from the Internet than from church history, more from their own intuition than formal study. When you wed the American independent streak with a postmodern skepticism toward institutions, you set the stage for what theologians call *syncretism*, which is the blending of elements from various faiths into a new form of spirituality. Like grazing at the buffet table at an all-you-can-eat cafeteria, *syncretists* adopt doctrines that seem appropriate to them and leave behind others they regard as offensive or outdated. What emerges is a Jesus customized for their worldview—a designer Jesus.

A 2005 survey by CBS disclosed that 36 percent of Americans combine the teachings of more than one religion into their own faith.[153] Thus, Los Angeles Lakers basketball coach Phil Jackson calls himself "a Zen Christian," while a well-known actress once identified herself as a Christian who is "into goddess worship." One Presbyterian minister described how he was taken aback when a woman introduced herself to him by saying, "I'm a Presbyterian Buddhist."[154]

The attitude of many Americans is that they like Jesus but not the church, which they see as exclusionary, condemning, intolerant, and intent on strapping people into a straitjacket of rigid beliefs. But the Jesus they like may look very different from the historical Jesus. If the traditional church imagines Jesus as a finely painted portrait, then syncretists often render him as abstract art—many times to the point where he's unrecognizable from the Jesus of ancient creeds.

Syncretism

The blending of sometimes-contradictory elements from various faiths into a new form of spirituality

For syncretists, that's okay. Many of them find their Jesus more satisfying than the judgmental Jesus they learned about in Sunday school. Besides, they assert, who's to say which Jesus is more "real" than the others? If history is all based on someone's interpretation, they reason, then nobody can be certain who Jesus was and what he taught anyway. In this age when "you have your truth, and I have mine," the important issue becomes what "works" for each individual life.

INTERVIEW #6: PAUL COPAN, PHD

My wife, Leslie, and I were chatting about these sorts of issues in my office one Saturday afternoon. The title of a book, crowded among many others on my shelves, caught her eye: *True for You, But Not for Me*. She pulled it out. "Maybe you ought to talk to the person who wrote this," she suggested as she handed the book to me.

I was familiar with the author, Paul Copan. When Leslie mentioned him, I remembered he's among the leading experts in this area. "That's a good idea," I said, and within days I'd made arrangements to fly to Florida and meet with him in his offices in West Palm Beach.

Copan and I sat down at a round wooden table in the corner

Bio: Paul Copan

- Chair of philosophy and ethics at Palm Beach Atlantic University
- Doctorate in philosophy from Marquette University
- Has taught at Trinity and Bethel seminaries
- Lecturer at Harvard, Boston College, State University of New York, and Moscow State University
- Author and editor of numerous books, articles, and reviews, including *True for You, But Not for Me*; *That's Just Your Interpretation*; and *How Do You Know You're Not Wrong?*
- Raises funds for microenterprise development loans in such countries as Nigeria, Peru, India, Mexico, Thailand, and Haiti

of his office, flanked by floor-to-ceiling shelves teeming with books. I started with a broad question to lay the foundation for our discussion. As I did so, I thought of Pontius Pilate's question two millennia ago: "What is truth?"[155]

IT'S ALL RELATIVE

"We're living in a postmodern era in which concepts like 'truth' and 'morality' are more elastic than in the past," I said to Copan. "How do you define postmodernism?"

"First, it's helpful to know what modernism involves," Copan said. "Modernism can be traced back to René Descartes, the 17th-century French philosopher who is famous for his pursuit of certainty. Descartes said that one thing he couldn't doubt was that he was thinking, so his starting point for knowledge became, 'I think, therefore, I am.' There was a sense in which you had to have 100 percent certainty or you couldn't know something," Copan continued.

"So postmodernism is a reaction to Descartes' quest for certainty and to the creation of systems like rationalism, romanticism, Marxism, Nazism, and scientism. These systems tend to oppress people who disagree with those in power—the Jews under Nazism and the capitalists under Marxism, for example. French philosopher Jean-François Lyotard said that, simplifying to the extreme, postmodernism is suspicion toward a 'metanarrative'—a 'big-picture' view of the world—that's taken to be true for all people in all cultures and which ends up oppressing people."

I was thinking through the implications as he was talking. "The idea, then, is that certainty leads to oppression?" I asked.

Postmodernism

A reaction to the quest for certainty and to the creation of systems like rationalism, romanticism, Marxism, Nazism, or scientism

"When people are so certain that they've got the truth and believe their system explains everything, then people who disagree with them are on the outside. They end up in Auschwitz or the Soviet gulags," he said. "So instead of 'meta-narratives,' postmodernism emphasizes 'mini-narratives.' In other words, each person has his or her own viewpoint or story."

"And each viewpoint is as valid as any other," I said, more of an observation than a question.

"That's the postmodern view, yes. There's a suspicion toward sweeping-truth claims, which are seen as power grabbing: Whoever is in charge can say 'This is true' and then back it up by oppressing those who disagree."

"And suspicion of truth can contribute, in some cases, to relativism," I commented.

"Right. To the relativist, no fact is true in all times and all places. The beliefs of a person are 'true' for him, but not necessarily for anyone else. This means that one person's 'truth,' which really amounts to his or her opinion, can directly conflict with another person's 'truth' and still be valid.

"To the relativist, no religion is universally or exclusively true. You can have your kind of Jesus, and I can have mine; it doesn't matter if our views contradict each other. There's no universal right and wrong. Moral values are true—or 'genuine'—for some, but not for others. Since there are different expressions of morality in the world, there's no reason to think that one viewpoint is any more true than another."

I searched my mind for an example. "So adultery can be okay for some people but not for others?" I asked.

Relativism

The belief nothing is true for all times and all places

"In the view of the relativist, yes," he replied. "Something is wrong only if *you* feel it's wrong. Now, relativists may not *approve* of adultery, and they may even have strong reservations about it. But they'll say, 'Who am I to say someone else is wrong?'"

"What are the greatest shortcomings of relativism?" I asked.

"Relativism falls apart logically when you examine it. As a worldview, it simply doesn't work," he said.

I was looking for specifics. "Tell me why," I said.

"For instance, relativists believe that relativism is true not just for them but for *every* person. They believe that relativism applies to nonrelativists ('true for *you*'), not just to themselves ('true for me'). The relativists find themselves in a bind if we ask them, 'Is relativism *absolutely* true for everyone?' To be consistent, the relativist must say, 'There's no reason to take seriously the claim that every belief is as good as every other belief, since this belief itself would be no better than any other.'"

Even so, I knew there must be reasons why postmodernism has taken root. "Are there aspects of postmodernism that make sense to you?" I asked.

"Despite some of its own incoherencies, yes, there are some lessons we can learn from it," he said. "For example, we *do* have our limitations, biases, and perspectives. We should admit that.

"Also, those with cultural or political power—even those with religious power—many times *do* try to spin the truth to suit their own agenda. And meta-narratives often *do* alienate and marginalize outsiders—although I should note that Christianity teaches the intrinsic value of every individual, including the disfranchised."

THE TRUTH ABOUT TRUTH

I went back to the infamous question posed by Pilate 2,000 years ago: "What *is* truth?"

I was expecting a complex answer heavy with philosophical jargon. Instead, Copan's definition was surprisingly straightforward: "I think people instinctively understand that truth is a belief, story, ideal, or statement that matches up with reality or corresponds to the way things really are."

When I asked him for an example, he said, "If I say the moon is made of cheese, that's false because it doesn't match up with the way things really are. Or consider an event in history: Martin Luther wrote out his 95 theses in 1517. That's factually true, and to disagree with that would mean that you believe something that's false."

Truth

A belief, story, ideal, or statement that matches up with reality or corresponds to the way things really are

He continued, "Something is true—or corresponds to reality—even if people don't believe it. I often use the example of the earth being round even when people thought it was flat. It wasn't as though people could fall over the edge of the earth and be swallowed by dragons back then. The earth was still round, even if people didn't believe it was."

"Some people," I observed, "believe that whatever *works* for them is true."

"Yes, that's the pragmatic view," he said, nodding in acknowledgment. "The problem is that people can have beliefs that are 'useful,' maybe temporarily and for certain ends, but they may also be completely false. And some things can be true—like the temperature at the North Pole—even though they don't help us in any way. So truth isn't merely what 'works.'

Pragmatist

Someone who takes a practical approach and is mainly concerned with what works

"On the other hand, the pragmatist does have a point when he asks, 'Can my beliefs be lived out practically?' If not, then it's highly likely that the view isn't true. What is true can be lived out consistently—there doesn't have to be a mismatch between 'theory' and 'practice.'

"Ultimately, it comes down to a theological question: Can there be an authoritative viewpoint? To put it in Christian terms: Is there the possibility of a special revelation in which God speaks authoritatively for all times and all cultures? Can God break onto the scene and offer a way to know truth with confidence?"

He allowed the question to hang in the air for a moment, then added: "Not only do I believe he *can*, but I believe he *has*."

THE "YUCK FACTOR"

Shifting the emphasis of my questions, I told Copan about Wendi and read this quote from her: "I don't believe in right or wrong. It just is. If it feels like something that I should do, then I'll do it." Turning to Copan, I asked, "What's the role of feelings in terms of what's true or false, right or wrong?"

"Feelings can be tricky," Copan began. "A person may say, 'I need to be true to myself by following my feelings'—and then run off with his secretary. Such people use their feelings to rationalize immoral behavior. The problem, of course, is that feelings are only one aspect of who we are. The capacity to feel is a God-given gift—but so is the capacity to think, to act in a morally responsible way, to discipline ourselves, and, by God's grace, to shape our character into something better than it presently is. If we follow only our feelings, then we're being false to *all* of who we are and what we were designed to be."

"Still," I countered, "there *is* a role for feelings."

"Absolutely. Feelings and intuition have their place. For instance, there's the 'yuck factor.'"

"The what?"

"The 'yuck factor' is when we don't even have to think through certain issues. We have a strong visceral revulsion against, say, rape or child abuse. We don't hem and haw by saying, 'Oh, well, maybe rape is right in some contexts.' We know immediately, on a gut level, that rape is wrong. This is evidence that there *are* objective moral values. They are valid and binding for everyone, not just for some cultures. And we should take intuitions about these moral values—the 'yuck factor'—seriously.

"In Romans 2, Paul says that even though Gentiles weren't given the law of Moses, their conscience bears witness, alternately accusing or else defending them, because the law has been placed in their hearts.[156] There is this moral law, and people with a well-functioning conscience can get a lot of things right.

"I wouldn't place complete reliance on feelings, though," Copan continued. "For example, what happens when feelings conflict? If you have a Jew in Nazi Germany who has certain feelings and you've got Hitler who has feelings the other way, then the person with the greater power wins out. But that doesn't make his actions right."

A MIX-AND-MATCH JESUS

"It seems like a lot of people are trying to free themselves from the straitjacket of religious dogma and create their own Jesus by picking and choosing what they want from Christianity and other faiths," I said. "What's wrong with creating our own Jesus to suit our own needs?"

"We should clarify that Christianity isn't primarily about subscribing to a set of teachings. Christianity is focused on the *person* of Christ. We're called into a relationship, not simply to believe a set of doctrines.

"The Scriptures are basically a narrative of God's interaction with humankind. If we lose this notion of God's desire for relationship with human beings, then we're in danger of losing the heart of the Christian faith. Doctrines, of course, will flow from that; but when the Scriptures call us to *believe*, we're being called to put our trust in *someone*, not just agree with a bunch of doctrine. Demons could do that. We are to commit ourselves to Christ."

"What about this tendency to pick and choose aspects of

other faiths and incorporate them into Christianity?" I asked.

"Well, if we *do* love God, then we want to follow his teachings. If Jesus *is* God's unique revelation to us, then we want to follow what he said and did. So certain doctrines flow naturally from that: Jesus' divinity, his death for our salvation, his resurrection, his command that we live righteous lives, and so forth. We shouldn't try to create our own Jesus or our own set of doctrines because then we are denying reality. Jesus reflects reality, so we need to align ourselves with him."

"If Jesus defines reality," I pressed, "then are you saying there's no truth in any other religion?"

"I believe there *are* some truths in other religions," he quickly replied. "As Scottish writer George MacDonald said, 'Truth is truth, whether from the lips of Jesus or Balaam.'[157] We need to affirm truth where we see it, but we also need to remember there are logical implications of certain beliefs. If you believe God exists, then you're going to have to reject certain aspects of, say, Buddhism—mainly, God's nonexistence. If you accept the existence of God, then large portions of Eastern philosophy are going to be wrong *at that point*. That doesn't mean they're 100 percent wrong, but they're wrong when they conflict with a view that is correct. You can't say, 'Well, I believe in Jesus' resurrection, but I also believe in reincarnation.' If it's true that Jesus really did rise from the dead, then reincarnation is not true. Human beings have one earthly opportunity and then face judgment.[158]

"If God has broken into the world and spoken through Christ, then there are going to be certain beliefs that we're going to have to accept. It's not up to us to say, 'I like this, I don't like that.' C. S. Lewis said he'd gladly get rid of the doctrine of hell, but he concluded he can't because there are certain things that flow from the claims of Christ and the teachings of the New Testament that precluded him from doing that. I think there needs to be that kind of honesty.

"We can say we find certain doctrines troubling—fine. But to try to pick and choose which doctrines we accept is denying the teachings of Jesus who—through his resurrection—has demonstrated the reliability of his claims about being the Son of God and thus knowing what's true and what isn't."[159]

REINCARNATION

Copan's mention of reincarnation turned my thoughts to a related line of inquiry. "So often, people who want to create their own religion will include the idea of reincarnation," I said. "Why is that?"

"Some people see reincarnation as another crack at life in order to get things right, sort of like the movie *Groundhog Day*. There's an attraction to saying we have many opportunities and not just one lifetime. Actually, the reality is quite different." He gestured toward me. "You've been to India, right?"

"I've spent some time there, yes," I said.

"I have, too. And I'm sure you've noticed that reincarnation is a very oppressive burden in that Hindu culture, as it is in the Buddhist world," he said. "For example, if you're a low caste or no caste Hindu, then you're stuck at that low level because that's what you deserve from your previous life. And people shouldn't reach out to help you because they might jeopardize their own karma by interfering with your living out the miserable existence that you deserve."

I knew he was right. What sounds on the surface like it gives people multiple opportunities to live a better life turns out to create a devastating situation for millions upon millions of people who are mired in hopeless poverty.

ARE WE ALL DIVINE?

Another belief that people frequently add to their customized faith is the idea that we're all divine. "What about this tendency to make ourselves God?" I asked. "Shirley MacLaine said, 'The tragedy of the human race was that we had forgotten that we were each Divine.'[160] Why do people tend to gravitate toward that conclusion?"

Copan smiled. "I would rewrite her statement by saying the tragedy of the human race is that we've forgotten we're God's creatures! *That's* the problem," he said, his tone lighthearted but emphatic at the same time. "Given a choice, we tend to select beliefs that elevate who we are, that diminish personal responsibility, that give us greater freedom to call 'good' what the Scriptures call 'sin,' and that put us in charge of our own destinies. We want to create guidelines that don't put any demands on us.

"We all know deep down that we're flawed and imperfect. What kind of god would that make us? We flatter ourselves when we try to put ourselves in the place of God rather than acknowledge that we are God's creation and that we need to give God his rightful place. We don't need to be more self-centered than we are; we need to be more God-centered. We can't find the real Jesus by thinking that we're his equal."

WHICH JESUS?

His comment about the "real Jesus" sparked a thought. "These days if someone says he believes in Jesus, you almost have to say, '*Which* Jesus?'" I observed.

"Unfortunately, that's true," he replied. "We're living in an age of biblical illiteracy, where a lot of people have cobbled-together beliefs of Jesus. But I can't stress this enough: *What we believe about Jesus doesn't really affect who he is,*" he said, his voice emphasizing each word.

That statement seemed pivotal. "Please, elaborate on that," I urged.

"Our beliefs can't change reality," he said. "Whether or not we choose to believe it, Jesus is the unique Son of God. How do we know? Because he convincingly demonstrated the trustworthiness of his remarkable claims through his resurrection. He is who he is, regardless of what we think. So we have a choice: We can live in a fantasyland of our own making by believing whatever we want about him; or we can seek to *discover* who he really is—and then bring ourselves into alignment with the real Jesus and his teachings."

THE JESUS OF HISTORY

Copan's conclusions about Jesus, of course, depend on whether he has an accurate assessment of what occurred in ancient history. Some postmodernists, however, contend that because history is a matter of interpretation, we can't be sure what really happened in the past. "The implication is clear," I said to Copan. "If we lack certainty about history, then one person's version of Jesus would be just as valid as anyone else's—or the church's."

"I think we need to make a distinction between *facts* and *interpretation*," Copan said. "We can know some facts with great confidence: For example, Hitler didn't overthrow the Roman Empire, or Stalin wasn't the first American president. We can know about the Reformation—Martin Luther posting his 95 theses in 1517, the Catholic Church's sale of indulgences, and so forth.

"The question comes at an interpretive level. Given the *facts* of history—which we can conclude from historical records, archaeology, and so forth—how do we put the historical picture together? Yes, there are going to be some differing interpretations, but it's not *all* a matter of interpretation. We can differentiate between more plausible interpretations and ones that are off-the-wall. Some explanations do a much better job of accounting for the historical facts—they're more comprehensive, they're better supported. So I simply reject the idea that we can't draw any conclusions based on history."

I brought the discussion back to Christ. "How much can we confidently know about Jesus?" I asked. "Is there enough historical data for us to have a sufficient understanding of who he is so we can reject interpretations that simply don't reflect reality?"

"We have excellent historical data concerning Jesus," was his quick response. "He is mentioned in writings outside the Bible, and we have lots of details in the New Testament, which holds up under examination very well."

Copan then detailed some of the points I'd already explored when I examined challenges to the trustworthiness of the New Testament. (See challenges #1 and #2.)

"But we can't have 100 percent confidence, can we?" I asked.

"Maybe not, but we have a very convincing picture that does a better job of explaining the facts than the competing theories. We can talk about the real Jesus of history as a unique individual who claims to stand in the place of God, who does remarkable things, who claims that in him the kingdom of God has come, and whose claims are vindicated by his resurrection and then corroborated by the conviction in the early church that he was the Son of God."

"Still, some people are very sincere in interpreting Jesus differently from the way the church traditionally has," I pointed out.

"I'll grant that they're sincere," Copan conceded. "Sincerity is important, but, Lee, we can't overlook this: *Sincerity is not sufficient.*

"Weren't Hitler and Stalin sincerely committed to their beliefs? I'm sure they were. But the idea that God would applaud their sincerity is absurd. Sometimes people can be very committed and seemingly sincere, but it's at the expense of suppressing their conscience. They've rejected and resisted the truth or suppressed their moral impulses."

"In other words," I suggested, "a person can be sincere but sincerely wrong."

"Exactly," Copan replied. "Sincerity doesn't make a person right. Sincerity doesn't make something true. I can sincerely believe that I'm every bit as divine as Jesus, but that doesn't change the fact that I'm a creature, not the Creator."

THE NEW TOLERANCE

Few things are as politically incorrect these days as saying that another person is wrong about his or her religious beliefs. Such a claim smacks of judgmentalism, which is to be avoided at all costs.

"Aren't you judging other people when you say they're wrong—and didn't Jesus say in Matthew 7:1, 'Do not judge, or you too will be judged'?" I asked Copan.

The mention of that verse brought a smile to his face. "That passage has replaced John 3:16 as the favorite verse that people like to quote," he said. "Unfortunately, though, many of them misinterpret what Jesus was saying. Jesus wasn't implying that we should never make judgments about people."

"How do you know?" I asked.

"Because in John 7:24, Jesus says, 'Stop judging by mere appearances, and make a right judgment.' So he's clarifying that it's all right—in fact, it's a good thing—to make *proper* judgments about people. What Jesus condemns is a critical and judgmental attitude or unholy sense of moral superiority.

"The Bible says in Galatians 6:1 that if a fellow Christian is caught in a sin, then those who are spiritual should seek to restore him or her 'in a spirit of gentleness. Look to yourself, lest you too be tempted.'[161] God wants us to examine ourselves first for the problems we so readily detect in other people. Only then should we seek to remove the speck in the other person's eye.[162] Making proper judgments is a good thing. What's bad is the ugly refusal to acknowledge that 'there but for the grace of God go I.'"

"So the key issue is our attitude?"

"Yes, that's right. We can hold our convictions firmly and yet treat people with dignity and respect even though they disagree with us. We can have a spirit of humility while at the same time explaining why we believe someone is wrong. Ephesians 4:15 talks about 'speaking the truth in love.' That should be our goal."

"It seems like *tolerance* has become the buzzword of the postmodern world," I remarked.

"Tolerance is a wonderful virtue—when it's properly defined. Its meaning, however, has become distorted in recent years."

"In what way?"

"Traditionally, to be tolerant meant putting up with what we find disagreeable or false. For example, some people will tolerate green beans when they're served them at a person's house. They'll eat them even though green beans aren't their favorite food. In the same way, tolerance has meant that we put up with people even though we disagree with their viewpoint.

"These days, though, tolerance means you accept the other person's views as being true or legitimate. If you claim that someone is wrong, you can be accused of being intolerant—even though, ironically, the person making the charge of intolerance isn't being accepting of *your* beliefs."

I thought of a Muslim acquaintance of mine who has come over to my house to grill steaks and discuss theology and history. We disagree on fundamental spiritual issues, but neither of us has drawn a knife on the other. We've found a way to be civil and respectful without pretending we agree on everything.

I shared that experience with Copan. "That's exactly what true tolerance is about," he said. "Dialogue shouldn't begin by assuming the equality of all *truth claims*, which is a ridiculous position. Instead, dialogue should begin with assuming the equality of all *persons*. True tolerance grants people the right to dissent."

ARROGANCE AND EXCLUSIVITY

Nevertheless, many people accuse Christians of being arrogant when they insist their religious beliefs are right while others' are wrong. I mentioned to Copan that theologian John Hick says all the world's religions are 'different culturally conditioned responses to the ultimately Real.'[163] In other words, religion is the imperfect attempt by human beings to understand the Ultimate Reality.

"That would mean that while all world religions express themselves differently, they all should be respected and none should claim to be better than another," I said.

Not surprisingly, Copan was well-versed in Hick's philosophy. "Religious pluralists like Hick believe all religions are capable of bringing salvation or liberation, and that this is evidenced by the moral fruits produced by those religions—people like Mahatma Gandhi and the Dalai Lama, for example," he explained. "But I think the pluralist is displaying the same arrogance he accuses Christians of having when Christians claim Jesus is the only way to God."

That statement intrigued me. "In what way?" I asked.

"The pluralist is saying that if you disagree with his viewpoint, then at that juncture you would be in error. He's saying the Christian is wrong and he's right. The pluralist believes his view ought to be accepted and the Christian's view rejected. So he's being as 'arrogant' as he accuses Christians of being. The pluralist is just as much of an exclusivist as the Christian."

I couldn't help but interrupt. "Yet aren't we culturally conditioned to some degree?" I asked. "Isn't it true that if you were born in Saudi Arabia, then you'd probably be a Muslim; or if you were born in India, then you'd probably be a Hindu?"

"Statistically speaking, that could be true," he said. "I could make the claim that if you lived in Nazi Germany, then chances are you would have been part of the Hitler Youth. Or if you lived in Stalin's Russia, you would have been a Communist. But does that mean Nazism or Communism is as good a political system as democracy?

"No. Just because there has been a diversity of political systems throughout history doesn't prevent us from concluding that one political system is superior to its rivals. Presumably, there are good reasons for preferring one political system over another. There are good reasons for rejecting a system like Nazism or Communism in favor of democracy. So why can't it be the same with regard to religious beliefs?

"The point is this: Are there good reasons for believing one religious viewpoint over another? I conclude, based on the historical evidence for Jesus' resurrection, that he has been vindicated as the true Son of God."

"I think what upsets some people is that there are certain Christians who sound morally superior when they talk about their faith," I observed.

"Yes, unfortunately that happens. But as Martin Luther said, when Christians are evangelizing, they're like one beggar simply telling another beggar where to find bread. It's not as though we are sharing the Christian faith from a position of moral superiority—like saying, 'I'm better than you because I'm a Christian and you're not.'

"Let me give you an example. My wife and I like a restaurant called Macaroni Grill. When we tell people about it, we're not saying, 'I'm better than you because I know about the Macaroni Grill and you don't.' No—we're merely happy to pass on the news about the place. And that's how it should be with the Christian faith. Our attitude shouldn't be, 'I'm better than you,' but 'I found something really good; I urge you to check it out.'"

JESUS AND THE MARGINALIZED

Even so, I still saw problems. "When one religion, like Christianity, claims a unique path to salvation, doesn't that inevitably lead to marginalizing and persecuting people who believe otherwise?" I asked.

"The question of *oppression* is a separate issue from that of *truth*. Does truth necessarily oppress? The people who hold to a truth can, but they don't have to. Religious people can oppress, but so can nonreligious people—look at Marxism and Stalinism. But is oppression consistent with what Jesus taught—the Jesus who sat down with the hated tax collectors, prostitutes, and the forgotten of society? Jesus actually came to the marginalized. He taught his followers to love all people. Christians may not always fully live out those principles, but this is the ideal Jesus tells us to strive for."

WHATEVER BECAME OF SIN?

One thing I've noticed among people who customize their own religion is that one of the first doctrines to go is sin. We may see ourselves as making mistakes, committing errors, or having a lapse of judgment, but few people envision themselves as sinners. We live in a blame-shifting culture where we tend to evade responsibility for our actions and point the finger at everyone else—especially society or our early childhood trauma—for our behavior.

I raised the issue with Copan. "If there is no such thing as sin anymore," I said, "then people wouldn't need a savior like the Jesus of the Bible, would they?"

"One of the problems of relativism is that it denies there's any moral standard to shoot for," he replied. "Consequently, there's no failure in meeting that standard—so then why, as you've asked, would you need a savior? Why do you need to be rescued? Why do you need redemption?

"But despite a lot of our therapeutic attempts to deal with human nature, the problem of evil in the human heart is something that keeps making realists of us. The Christian faith talks about human sinfulness and rebellion against God, which we can readily see demonstrated throughout the world."

To make sure we were both using the same terminology, I asked, "What's the biblical definition of *sin*?"

"The Westminster Confession talks about sin being the lack of conformity to, or any kind of transgression of, the law of God. Basically, it's a violation of the character of God. It's something that falls short of what God desires for us. I guess if you want to put it in contemporary jargon, *sin* is doing whatever you want. *Sin* is having attitudes that are self-absorbed and self-centered, rather than being God-centered.

"But the fact that we are born with a self-centered tendency is not the whole story. There's also the story of redemption — that Christ has come to bring relief and resolution to a problem that, when left to ourselves, we simply aren't able to address."

COSMIC CHILD ABUSE?

That brought me to my next topic. "Christians say Jesus died on the cross to pay for their sins, but is this concept of the substitutionary atonement outdated?" I asked. "Episcopal Bishop John Shelby Spong said, 'A human father who would nail his son to a cross for any purpose would be arrested for child abuse.'"[164]

Substitutionary Atonement
The teaching that Jesus died as a substitute for sinners

"We have to be careful about viewing this notion as being outmoded," came Copan's reply. "C. S. Lewis rightly warns us against what he called 'chronological snobbery'—saying, 'Oh, they used to do things that way, but we know better now because we're more enlightened.' Sometimes there is a mindset that claims if no one believes something anymore, then surely it has to be false. The question should be: Is there anything to this notion of substitutionary atonement?"

"Well, *is* there?" I asked. "Why can't God just say he forgives the sins of the world?"

Copan's answer came swiftly. "Why can't judges just forgive criminals? Why can't they let rapists and thieves back on the street and just say, 'It's okay. I forgive you'? For God to do something like this would be an insult to his holiness. He is a righteous judge, and therefore he must find us guilty of sin because the truth of the matter is we *are* guilty. We have fallen short of how God wants us to live. We violate even our own moral standards, so certainly we violate God's higher standard. To pretend otherwise would be a lie—and God is not a liar.

"Also, if God simply forgives, then he hasn't taken human responsibility with much seriousness at all. To simply let people go does not hold them accountable to the standards that people know they've transgressed. And he would be denying the gravity of sin—which we take far too lightly, but which God takes very, very seriously."

That last remark made me think of a comment I'd read in a book during the plane ride to Florida. As James R. Edwards, a professor of biblical languages and literature, as well as a Presbyterian minister, said in his book *Is Jesus the Only Savior?*—

The doctrine of atonement obviously hangs on the doctrine of sin. A physician who removes a leg because of a splinter is a monster. A physician who removes a leg because of cancer or gangrene, on the other hand, is a hero who saves his or her patient's life. It all depends on the nature and seriousness of the problem. Spong and others see sin as a splinter; the New Testament sees it as a cancer that is fatal if left untreated. And that accounts for the sacrifice of Jesus Christ on a cross of cruelty and shame. The cross is indeed an outrage—an outrage of grace. If this is the kind of world in which we live—and I believe it is—then the death of God's Son for the sins of the world is the *only* way the world can be reunited with its Maker and Redeemer.[165]

"There's a cost to sin," Copan pointed out. "Romans 6:23 says it's death, or eternal separation from God.[166] That's the penalty we owe. That's the cost we incur when our sins separate us from God. But Jesus willingly paid the price in our place, as our substitute—and he offers forgiveness as a free gift.

"God isn't guilty of cosmic child abuse. It's not as though the Father consigns the Son to this humiliating death on the cross; it's something Jesus does voluntarily. Jesus says in John 10 that he lays down his life of his own accord.[167] This is something the Son willingly takes upon himself in order to pay the debt that humankind could not pay on its own.

"So what should our response be? *Gratitude*—the Christian faith is a religion of gratitude. Why would we be reluctant to humble ourselves and receive the free gift of forgiveness that Christ purchased through his death—and also receive the Gift-Giver himself as the Leader of our life?"

SOLO SPIRITUALITY

Copan's description of Jesus' sacrifice was moving. Yet love and grace isn't always the message people hear from Christians. I quoted to Copan the words of emergent church leader Dan Kimball: "Today, Christians are known as scary, angry, judgmental, right-wing finger-pointers with political agendas."[168]

I asked Copan, "In light of that, isn't it understandable that people wouldn't want to hear about the Jesus that Christians believe in?"

"Absolutely," Copan said. "Jesus said in John 13:35, 'By this all men will know that you are my disciples, if you love one another.' Well, frankly, we can look around and see a lot of people who are not acting like Jesus' disciples. Instead of being able to say, 'Yes, look at us Christians and how we're living exemplary lives,' many times we have to say, 'Sorry, look at Jesus, not at us.' At the same time, though, some people can use this as an excuse not to take Jesus seriously."

I noted to Copan that the title of Kimball's book sums up the attitude of many people today: *They Like Jesus but Not the Church*. As Bono said: "I'm not often comfortable in church. It feels pious and so unlike the Christ that I read about in the Scriptures."[169]

"As a result," I said, "spirituality is very individualistic for a lot of people. They say they can worship God better while walking alone in the woods than in church. Can a Christian be independent from Christian community?"

"Frankly, you can't live out the Christian life—with all of its commands about dealing with 'one another'—without be-

ing part of the church," Copan replied. "As the author of Hebrews says, we need to stimulate one another to love and good
works. He says we shouldn't abandon gathering together as believers.[170] The church isn't perfect, but then neither are we as
individuals."

"So solo spirituality is not something you'd recommend?"
I asked.

"No, certainly not. Despite all of our failures, we cannot live
the Christian life apart from one another. In fact, the fruit of
the Holy Spirit—love, joy, peace, patience, kindness, goodness,
faithfulness, gentleness, and self-control—requires community
living.[171] These are community virtues that need to be cultivated
in a way that can't be accomplished in isolation."

THE RADICAL JESUS

"What lessons can we learn from postmodernism?" I asked.

"Postmodernism rightly reminds us that we have a certain
historical context, that we don't always see things clearly, and
so forth. But even though we may not know everything, we
can know *some* things—indeed, some very important and life-
changing things," Copan insisted. "We can know enough to encounter and experience the real Jesus."

My mind flashed to the countless people who've discon-
nected Jesus from reality and then manufactured their own version of him—a Jesus who teaches them what they want to hear,
rather than what they desperately need to know. This Jesus is
anemic—powerless and pale—because he exists only in their
imaginations. All the while, the authentic Jesus—with his love
and strength, his miraculous power and saving grace—stands
patiently by.

I began to feel a sense of sadness. "Isn't it a shame," I said to Copan, "that so many people are creating a Jesus who matches their preconceptions about what they think he should be like, but in the process, they're missing the real Jesus?"

Copan nodded in agreement. "Ironically, they're often talking about a 'radical new Jesus' they've discovered. *Radical?*" he repeated, incredulous. "No, these are silly or watered-down portrayals of Jesus. He's more than a good buddy, more than a social revolutionary, more than a Gnostic teacher. The real Jesus is the Jesus of orthodox Christianity: *He's no less than God incarnate.* God breaks into the world scene with Jesus. He conquers sin, Satan, and death through Jesus. He's bringing history to a climax through Jesus. *This* is what humankind has been waiting for.

"If you want a spectacular Jesus, or a hero for the ages, or a Jesus who shatters all expectations and pours out love beyond comprehension—there he is," he declared, thumping the table with his hand.

"How in the world can you get more radical than that?"

Discovering
the Real Jesus

She was brought up Catholic, but by the age of 18, she'd left the church and abandoned her belief in God. Two years later, she married a fervent atheist. Soon she became not just a published novelist, but also one of the best-read authors in America, penning a succession of stories about vampires and witches—unaware her books "reflected my quest for meaning in a world without God."[172]

Anne Rice, author of *Interview with the Vampire* and the Mayfair Witches series, was an atheist for 30 years. Then she began studying the Bible during her frequent periods of depression. Her faith rekindled, she decided in 2002 to "give myself utterly to the task of trying to understand Jesus himself and how Christianity emerged." She consecrated her subsequent book on Jesus—and herself—to him. And that's when she discovered something very curious.

An inveterate researcher, Rice prides herself on the accuracy of the historical world she creates for her novels. To prepare for writing about Jesus, she spent more than two years delving deeply into first-century Palestine, which included reading books on the New Testament era written by skeptical historians.

"I expected to discover that their arguments would be frighteningly strong, and that Christianity was, at heart, a kind of fraud," she wrote. Surprisingly, the opposite occurred:

> What gradually came clear to me was that many of the skeptical arguments—arguments that insisted most of the Gospels were suspect, for instance, or written too late to be eyewitness accounts—lacked coherence.... Arguments about Jesus himself were full of conjecture. Some books were no more than assumptions piled upon assumptions. Absurd conclusions were reached on the basis of little or no data at all.

In short, she found the nondivine and impotent Jesus of liberal circles to be based on "some of the worst and most biased scholarship I've ever read." She was stunned that "there are New Testament scholars who detest and despise" the Jesus they've spent their entire lives studying. "Some pitied him as a hopeless failure," she said. "Others sneered at him, and some felt an outright contempt. This came between the lines of the books."

In the end, she became "disillusioned with the skeptics and with the flimsy evidence for their conclusions." Instead, she discovered that the research and arguments from a wide range of other highly credentialed scholars—Richard Bauckham, Craig Blomberg, N. T. Wright, Luke Timothy Johnson, D. A. Carson, Larry Hurtado, and others—were more than enough to establish the early dating and first-person witness of the Gospels.

For years, skeptical and left-leaning historians have bedazzled the public with flashy new theories about Jesus—he's really a Gnostic imparter of secret wisdom; he's actually a reworking of the ancient myths about Mithras; he's a messianic pretender who fails the test of the ancient prophecies; or he's whatever anyone wants him to be in today's cacophony of postmodernism.

"These skeptical scholars," said Rice, "seemed so very sure of themselves."

Very sure—but as it turns out, they were surely wrong. The truth is that skepticism does not equal scholarship. Finally, other scholars are beginning to speak up to expose the leaps of logic, special pleading, biased interpretations, and tissue-thin evidence that underlie these outrageous claims about Jesus.

ANSWERING THE CHALLENGES

After traveling a total of 24,000 miles on my mission to investigate six of the most current and controversial objections to the traditional view of Jesus, I went alone to my office, sat down in a comfortable chair, and flipped through reams of notes, transcripts, and articles.

In the end, none of these seemingly daunting challenges turned out to be close calls. One by one, they were systematically dismantled by scholars who backed up their positions not with verbal tricks or speculation, but with facts, logic, and evidence:

- *Are scholars uncovering a radically different Jesus through ancient documents that are just as credible as the four Gospels?* No, the alternative texts are too late to be historically credible—for instance, the Gospel of Thomas was written after AD 175 and probably closer to 200. The Secret Gospel of Mark, with its homoerotic undercurrents, turned out to be an embarrassing hoax that fooled many scholars who were too eager to buy into bizarre theories about Jesus. No serious historians give credence to the so-called *Jesus Papers*. And the Gnostic depiction of Jesus as a revealer of hidden knowledge lacks any connection to the historical Jesus.

- *Is the Bible's portrait of Jesus unreliable because of mistakes or deliberate changes made by scribes through the centuries?* No, there are no new disclosures that have cast any doubt on the essential reliability of the New Testament. Only about 1 percent of the manuscript variants affect the meaning of the text to some degree and have a decent chance of going back to the original—and not a single central doctrine is at stake. Actually, the unrivaled wealth of New Testament manuscripts greatly enhances the credibility of the Bible's portrayal of Jesus.

- *Have new explanations refuted Jesus' resurrection?* No, the truth is that a persuasive case for Jesus rising from the dead can be made by using five facts that are well-evidenced and which the vast majority of today's scholars on the subject— including skeptical ones—accept as true: the fact that Jesus was killed by crucifixion; the fact that his disciples believed he rose and appeared to them; the conversion of the church persecutor Paul; the conversion of the skeptic James, who was Jesus' half-brother; and Jesus' empty tomb. All of the skeptics' attempts to put Jesus back into his tomb utterly fail when subjected to serious analysis.

- *Were Christian beliefs about Jesus stolen from pagan religions?* No, they clearly were not. Allegations that the virgin birth and the resurrection came from earlier mythology evaporated when the shoddy scholarship of "copycat" theorists was exposed. There are simply no examples of dying and rising gods that preceded Christianity and that have meaningful parallels to Jesus' resurrection. In short, this is a theory that careful scholars discredited decades ago.

- *Was Jesus an impostor who failed to fulfill the prophecies about the Messiah?* On the contrary, a compelling case can be made that Jesus—and Jesus alone—matches the "fingerprint" of the Messiah. Only Jesus managed to fulfill the prophecies that needed to come to fruition prior to the fall of the Jewish temple in AD 70. If Jesus isn't the predicted Messiah, then there will never be one. What's more, Jesus' fulfillment of these prophecies against all odds makes it reasonable to believe he will also fulfill the final prophesies when the time is right.

- *Should people be free to pick and choose what they want to believe about Jesus?* Obviously, we have the freedom to believe anything we want. But just because the U.S. Constitution provides equal protection for all religions, that doesn't mean all beliefs are equally true. Whatever we believe about Jesus cannot change the reality of who he clearly established himself to be: The unique Son of God. So why cobble together our own make-believe Jesus to try to fulfill our personal prejudices when we can meet and experience the actual Jesus of history and faith?

FOLLOWING THE UNIQUE JESUS

Not only had the six challenges been answered, but my journey had also yielded a fresh and powerful affirmative case for the overall reliability of the four Gospels, Jesus' fulfillment of the messianic predictions, and his resurrection. For me, it was further confirmation that the traditional view of Christ is amply supported by a firm foundation of historical facts.

Yet if that case is so convincing, then why do so many critics rely on flimsy evidence and feeble arguments in order to build a much weaker case for a fabricated Jesus? For instance, why would they ignore or belittle the first-century, eyewitness-based Gospels of the New Testament and instead manufacture a different Jesus out of second-century—or later—documents that lack historical credibility?

It's not always easy to discern people's motives. Still, I can't help but notice a common thread that runs through these efforts to discover another Jesus: Many of them, in their own way, attempt to put humankind on the same level as God.

Some critics try to accomplish this by reducing Jesus. They reject his uniqueness, his miracles, and his divinity, transforming him into just another human being. This is the tactic employed by the Jesus Seminar, advocates of the "copycat" theory, and the skeptics who deny the resurrection. It's the message behind the now-discredited *Jesus Papers:* Jesus never claimed to be God but only embodied God's Spirit in a way that anyone could.

Others take a different approach: Rather than tearing Jesus down, they elevate themselves. In other words, they're fine with affirming the divinity of Jesus—as long as they too are indwelled by the same spark of the divine. This seems to be the strategy of many new agers and Gnostics, as well as the people who set out to create their own do-it-yourself religion, only to "discover" that they're gods themselves.

Whether reducing Jesus or elevating ourselves, the result is the same: Jesus becomes our equal. As such, he doesn't deserve our allegiance or our worship. He cannot judge us or hold us accountable. His teachings become mere suggestions that can be followed or disregarded according to our whims. He isn't our Savior; at most, he's a friendly guide.

On the other hand, the one Jesus that skeptics refuse to tolerate is a uniquely divine, miraculous, prophecy-fulfilling, and resurrected Jesus—even if the historical evidence points persuasively in that direction. After all, that would put them in the place of being beholden to him. Their personal superiority and moral independence would be at risk. The problem is this: *That's* the real Jesus.

We are not his equals. We don't occupy the same stratum or possess the same status. He is God, and we're not. For many people, that's the crux of their predicament: If Jesus is God incarnate, then he might demand too much. And in fact, he does demand *everything*. Said C. S. Lewis,

> The Christian way is different: harder, and easier. Christ says, "Give me All. I don't want so much of your time and so much of your money and so much of your work: I want You. I have not come to torment your natural self, but to kill it. No half-measures are any good.... Hand over the whole natural self, all the desires which you think innocent as well as the ones you think wicked—the whole outfit. I will give you a new self instead. In fact, I will give you Myself: my own will shall become yours."[173]

That kind of surrender sounds scary for many people. But if Jesus actually is God—if he really did sacrifice himself so we could be forgiven and set free to experience his love forever—then why should we hesitate to give all of ourselves to him? Who could be more trustworthy than someone who lays down his life so that others might live? This is what Jesus has done. The church has been telling this same story for two millennia.

As I sat in my office, I found Craig Evans' words echoing in my mind: "I come down on the side of the church," he declared. "Doggone it, bless their bones, I think they figured it out. They avoided errors and pitfalls to the left and to the right. I think the church got it right."

As imperfect as she is, the church has preserved for us the four Gospels that constitute the most reliable reports about Jesus. The church has formulated the ancient creeds that efficiently sum up the implications of his life and ministry: Jesus is fully God and fully man, who offers forgiveness, hope, and eternal life as a free gift to all who want to receive it.[174]

As the church has affirmed from the beginning, Jesus is utterly one of a kind.

This is the *real* Jesus, who all along has been alive and well as he dwells in the lives of his people—the community whose door is always open...even to you.

Helpful Web Sites to Investigate the Real Jesus

LeeStrobel.com

...a video-intensive site that explores what Christians believe about Christianity—and why. Also available is Lee's free blog and e-newsletter, Investigating Faith.

JesusCentral.com

...a place to learn and dialogue about what Jesus said.

Reasonablefaith.org

...an articulate defense of biblical Christianity by scholar William Lane Craig.

Tektonics.org

...a feisty site that answers critics of historic Christianity.

Christian-thinktank.com

...a vast resource of answers to current objections to Christianity.

Markdroberts.com

...a wealth of material from the Harvard-educated scholar.

Willowcreek.com

...includes a guide to finding local churches that can help in your spiritual journey.

Whoisjesus-really.com

...provides answers to top questions concerning Christianity

Metamorpha.com

...where the focus is on how to become more like Jesus.

NOTES

Introduction

1. Doyle P. Johnson, "Dilemmas of Charismatic Leadership: The Case of the People's Temple," *Sociological Analysis* 40 (1979): 320.

2. See Sally Quinn and Jon Meacham, "Who Was Jesus?" available at www.newsweek.washingtonpost.com/onfaith/2006/12/who_was_jesus/comments.html#760080 (Dec. 26, 2006). The bulleted points are condensed from the submissions, but they preserve the author's original language as much as possible.

3. See Neil Gross and Solon Simmons, "How Religious Are America's College and University Professors?" available at www.wjh.harvard.edu/soc/faculty/gross/religions.pdf (Oct. 22, 2006).

4. Jesus said in John 8:24: "I told you that you would die in your sins; if you do not believe that I am [he], you will indeed die in your sins."

Challenge #1

5. The reporters who broke the story, which won first place for investigative reporting among Illinois newspapers from United Press International in 1986, were Anne Burris, Thomas J. Lee, Pete Nenni, Chris Szechenyi, and Kathy Schaeffer.

6. See Robert J. Miller, ed., *The Complete Gospels* (Santa Rosa, Calif.: Polebridge, revised and expanded edition, 1994).

7. Ibid., back cover.

8. Ibid., 3.

9. Gregory A. Boyd, *Jesus Under Siege* (Wheaton, Ill.: Victor, 1995), 14.

10. Philip Jenkins, *Hidden Gospels* (Oxford: Oxford University Press, 2001), 7.

11. Ibid., 357.

12. Morton Smith, *The Secret Gospel* (Middletown, Calif.: Dawn Horse, reissued 2005), 107.

13. Michael Baigent, *The Jesus Papers* (San Francisco: HarperSanFrancisco, 2006), 270.

14. All interviews have been edited for conciseness, clarity, and content. Interviews in this book have been adapted and condensed from *The Case for the Real Jesus*.

15 See Nicholas Perrin, Thomas and Tatian: *The Relationship between the Gospel of Thomas and the Diatessaron*, Academia Biblica 5 (Atlanta: Society of Biblical Literature, 2002); Nicholas Perrin, "NHC II,2 and the Oxyrhynchus Fragments (P.Oxy 1, 654, 655): Overlooked Evidence for a Syriac Gospel of Thomas," Vigiliae Christianae 58 (2004): 138-51; and Nicholas Perrin, *Thomas, the Other Gospel* (Louisville: Westminster John Knox Press, 2007).

16 Ben Witherington III, *The Gospel Code* (Downers Grove, Ill.: InterVarsity, 2004), 75.

17 Philip Jenkins, *Hidden Gospels* (Oxford: Oxford University Press, 2001), 17.

18 See Lee Strobel and Garry Poole, *Exploring the Da Vinci Code* (Grand Rapids, Mich.: Zondervan, 2006).

19 See Stephen C. Carlson, *The Gospel Hoax: Morton Smith's Invention of Secret Mark* (Waco, Texas: Baylor University Press, 2005).

20 Irenaeus, *Against Heresies* 1.31.1.

21 "In my vision at night I looked, and there before me was one like a son of man, coming with the clouds of heaven. He approached the Ancient of Days and was led into his presence. He was given authority, glory and sovereign power; all nations and peoples of every language worshiped him. His dominion is an everlasting dominion that will not pass away, and his kingdom is one that will never be destroyed" (Daniel 7:13-14).

Challenge #2

22 Bart D. Ehrman, *Misquoting Jesus* (San Francisco: HarperSanFrancisco, 2005), 7.

23 Emphasis added.

24 See www.csntm.org.

25 See www.bible.org.

26 2 Timothy 3:16-17—"All Scripture is God-breathed and is useful for teaching, rebuking, correcting and training in righteousness, so that the man of God may be thoroughly equipped for every good work."

27 See Matthew 1:22; 2:15.

28 Ehrman, *Misquoting Jesus*, 207-8.

29 See John 7:53-8:11.

30 Shawntaye Hopkins, "Woman Bitten by Snake at Church Dies," *Lexington Herald-Leader* (Nov. 8, 2006).

31 Frank R. Zindler, "The Real Bible: Who's Got It?" (May 1986) www.atheists.org/christianity/realbible.html (Nov. 29, 2006).

32 See Michael Baigent, Richard Lee, and Henry Lincoln, *Holy Blood, Holy Grail* (New York: Dell, 1983), 368-69.

33 Ehrman, *Misquoting Jesus*, Acknowledgments.

34 For the entire interview with Metzger, see Lee Strobel, *The Case for Christ* (Grand Rapids, Mich.: Zondervan, 1998), 55-72.

Challenge #3

35 See Strobel, *The Case for Christ*, 191-257.

36 See Surah 4:157-58.

37 Lemuel Lall, "Jesus Christ Lived in India, was buried in Kashmir: RSS Chief," wwrn.org/article.php?idd=24077

38 Robert M. Price and Jeffrey Jay Lowder, eds., *The Empty Tomb* (Amherst, N.Y.: Prometheus, 2005), 16.

39 John Dominic Crossan, *Jesus: A Revolutionary Biography* (San Francisco: HarperCollins, 1991), 145.

40 James D. Tabor, *The Jesus Dynasty* (New York: Simon & Schuster, 2006), 230 (emphasis in original).

41 Tacitus, Annals 15.44.

42 Josephus, *Antiquities* 18.64.

43 See Acts 9:26-30; 15:1-35.

44 1 Corinthians 15:3-7.

45 Dean John Rodgers of Trinity Episcopal School for Ministry, quoted in Richard N. Ostling, "Who Was Jesus?" Time, Aug. 15, 1988.

46 Irenaeus, *Against Heresies*, 3.3.4.

47 Polycarp's letter to the Philippians 9:2. Translation by Gary Habermas and Michael Licona.

48 Gerd Lüdemann, *What Really Happened to Jesus?* trans. John Bowden (Louisville: Westminster John Knox, 1995), 80.

49 See 1 Corinthians 9:1 and 15:8; Acts 9; 22; and 26.

50 See Matthew 12:46-50; 13:55-56; Mark 3:31-35; 6:3; Luke 8:19-21; John 2:12; 7:3, 5, 10; Acts 1:13-14; 1 Corinthians 9:5; Galatians 1:19.

51 See Mark 3:21; 6:3-4; and John 7:3-5.

52 John 7:3-5—"Jesus' brothers said to him, 'You ought to leave here and go to Judea, so that your disciples may see the miracles you do. No one who wants to become a public figure acts in secret. Since you are doing these things, show yourself to the world.' For even his own brothers did not believe in him."

53 See Acts 15:12-21 and Galatians 1:18-20.

54 See Josephus (Antiquities 20:200); Hegesippus (quoted by Eusebius in EH 2:23); *Clement of Alexandria* (quoted by Eusebius in EH 2:1, 23).

55 Reginald Fuller, *The Formation of the Resurrection Narratives* (New York: Macmillan, 1971), 37.

56 Acts 2:32.

57 Talmud, *Sotah* 19a.

58 Talmud, *Rosh Hashannah* 1.8

59 Josephus, *Antiquities* 4.8.15.

60 Abdullah Yusuf Ali, translator, *The Qur'an* (Elmhurst, N.Y.: Tahrike Tarsile Qur'an, Inc., 1999), 61.

61 Baigent, *The Jesus Papers*, 125.

62 Ibid., 130 (emphasis added).

63 Carrier, "The Spiritual Body of Christ," in Price and Lowder, eds., *Empty Tomb*, 184.

64 Strobel, *The Case for Christ*, 238.

65 See Deuteronomy 21:23.

66 Carrier, "The Spiritual Body of Christ," in Price and Lowder, eds., *Empty Tomb*, 156.

67 Uta Ranke-Heinemann, *Putting Away Childish Things* (San Francisco: HarperSanFrancisco, 1994), 131.

68 Paul Copan and Ronald K. Tacelli, eds., *Jesus' Resurrection: Fact or Figment?* (Downers Grove, Ill.: InterVarsity, 2000), 44.

69 Jeffery Jay Lowder, "Historical Evidence and the Empty Tomb Story," in Price and Lowder, eds., *Empty Tomb*, 267.

70 Acts 2:32.

71 Robert M. Price, "By This Time He Stinketh," in Price and Lowder, eds., *Empty Tomb*, 423.

72 Jeffery Jay Lowder, "Historical Evidence and the Empty Tomb Story," in Price and Lowder, eds., *Empty Tomb*, 288.

73 See Francis S. Collins, *The Language of God* (New York: Free Press, 2006), especially 11-31 and 213-25.

Challenge #4

74 See Helen Keller, *The Story of My Life*, Chapter XIV, www.afb.org/MyLife/book. asp?ch=P1Ch14 (Jan. 23, 2007).

75 Law.com defines *plagiarism* as "Taking the writings or literary concepts (a plot, characters, words) of another and selling and/or publishing them as one's own product." See dictionary.law.com.

76 Dan Brown, *The Da Vinci Code* (New York: Doubleday, 2003), 232.

77 See J. P. Holding, "Did the Mithraic Mysteries Influence Christianity?" www.tektonics. org/copycat/mithra.html (Jan. 23, 2007).

78 Tim Callahan, *Secret Origins of the Bible* (Altadena, Calif.: Millennium, 2002), 332.

79 See Challenge #3.

80 Tryggve N. D. Mettinger, *The Riddle of Resurrection* (Stockholm: Almqvist & Wicksell, 2001), 221.

81 Ibid.

82 Ibid.

83 See Strobel, *The Case for Christ*, 73-91.

84 See Manfred Clauss, (tranms. Richard Gordon) *The Roman Cult of Mithras* (New York: Routledge, 2000), 14-15, 21-22, 28.

85 See Jonathan David, "The Exclusion of Women in the Mithraic Mysteries: Ancient or Modern?" Numen 47 (2000), 121-41.

86 Manfred Clauss (translated by Richard Gordon), *The Roman Cult of Mithras*, 7.

87 L. Patterson, *Mithraism and Christianity* (Cambridge: Cambridge University Press, 1921), 94.

88 See Gary Lease, "Mithraism and Christianity: Borrowings and Transformations," in: Wolfgang Haase, ed., *Aufstieg und Niedergang der Römischen Welt, Vol. II* (Berlin/New York: Walter de Gruyter, 1980), 1321-22.

89 See Edwin M. Yamauchi, *Persia and the Bible* (Grand Rapids, Mich.: Baker, paperback edition, 1996), 520-21.

90 Richard Gordon, *Image and Value in the Greco-Roman World* (Aldershot: Variorum, 1996), 96, quoted in J. P. Holding, "Did the Mithraic Mysteries Influence Christianity?"

91 See Romans 6:3.

92 E. J. Yarnold, "Two Notes on Mithraic Liturgy," Mithras: Bulletin of the Society for Mithraic Studies (1974), 1.

93 See Luke 1:1-4.

94 Robert J. Miller, *Born Divine* (Santa Rosa, Calif.: Polestar, 1993), 246.

95 For a discussion of the Isaiah 7:14 prophecy, see Challenge #5.

96 Robert Gromacki, *The Virgin Birth* (Grand Rapids, Mich.: Kregel, second edition, 2002), 213.

97 See Barry B. Powell, *Classical Myth* (Upper Saddle River, N.J.: Prentice Hall, third edition, 2001), 250. To examine artwork of the birth of Dionysus on an Italian vase, circa 380 BC, showing him emerging from Zeus' thigh, see 251. According to J. Ed Komoszewski, M. James Sawyer, and Daniel B. Wallace, any reference to a "virgin birth" for Dionysus comes in post-Christian sources. See Komoszewski, Sawyer, and Wallace, *Reinventing Jesus*, 242-43.

98 See Edwin M. Yamauchi, "Anthropomorphism in Ancient Religions," *Bibliotheca Sacra* 125 (1968): 99.

99 J. Gresham Machen, *The Virgin Birth of Christ* (Grand Rapids, Mich.: Baker, 1965, reprint of Harper & Row edition, 1930), 326.

100 Peter Green, *Alexander of Macedon* (Berkeley: University of California Press, 1991), 37.

101 Buddha lived about 500 years before Christ. As Machen notes: "In the introduction to the JÐtaka book, which dates from the fifth century after Christ, we have the well-known story of the white elephant that entered into the body of MÐyÐ, Buddha's mother, at the time when her child was conceived; and the white elephant story seems to be shown by inscriptional evidence to have been current as early as the reign of Asoka in the third century before Christ. In its earliest form, the story appears as the narration of a dream; dreamed that a marvelous white elephant entered into her side.... In later Buddhist sources, what had originally been regarded as a dream of MÐyÐ came to be regarded as an actual happening.... It would be difficult to imagine anything more unlike the New Testament story of the virgin birth of Christ." See Machen, *The Virgin Birth of Christ*, 339-41 (emphasis in original).

102 See Edwin M. Yamauchi, "Historical Notes on the (In)comparable Christ," *Christianity Today* (Oct. 22, 1971).

103 See "Story of Lord Krishna's Birth," Sanatan Sanstha: *Sanatan Society for Scientific Spirituality*, www.sanatan.org/en/campaigns/KJ/birth.htm (Jan. 28, 2007).

104 Quoted in Tom Snyder, *Myth Conceptions* (Grand Rapids, Mich.: Baker, 1995), 194.

105 2 Peter 1:16.

Challenge #5

106 Brickner quotations are from: Sarah Pulliam, "'Volcanic' Response: Jews for Jesus Takes to New York City Streets," *Christianity Today* (Sept. 2006).

107 Michael Luo, "Jews for Jesus Hit Town and Find a Tough Crowd," *New York Times* (July 4, 2006).

108 Pulliam, "'Volcanic' Response."

109 "I Won't Fall Prey to Jews for Jesus," *New York Daily News* (July 12, 2006).

110 Joshua Waxman, "The Limits of Identity," in "The Virtual Talmud," blog.beliefnet. com/virtualtalmud/2006/08/limits-of-identity.html#more]

111 Aryeh Kaplan, *The Real Messiah?* (Toronto: Jews for Judaism, 2004), 14.

112 See J. Barton Payne, *Encyclopedia of Biblical Prophecy* (New York: Harper & Row, 1973).

113 See John 4:25-26.

114 Kaplan, *The Real Messiah?* 4, 14.

115 See Mark 14:62.

116 The NIV translates Isaiah 52:13: "See, my servant will act wisely; he will be raised and lifted up and highly exalted."

117 See Deuteronomy 4:12, 15, 36; 6:4; Isaiah 43:10-11; 45:5-6; 46:9.

118 See Exodus 33:20.

119 See Genesis 32:30.

120 See Isaiah 6:1.

121 John 1:18 (RSV).

122 John 10:30.

123 See John 10:36.

124 See Colossians 2:9.

125 Kaplan, *The Real Messiah?*, 16.

126 "Do All Scholars Believe Jesus Fulfilled Messianic Prophecies?" www.whoisthisjesus. tv/qa.htm#scholars (Dec. 28, 2006).

127 Ibid.

128 The prophecies foretold that several things had to occur before the second temple was destroyed in AD 70, including the bringing of everlasting atonement, or the final dealing with sin (see Daniel 9:24) and God filling the temple with his glory, which can only apply to his presence (see Haggai 2:6-9). The prophet Malachi said the Lord will come to his temple, purifying some of his people and bringing judgment on others (see Malachi 3:1-5). "So it's not a matter of maybe there's another one who's the Messiah," said Brown. "If it's not Yeshua, then throw out the Bible because nobody except him accomplished what needed to be done prior to AD 70."

129 Jews for Judaism, Missionary Impossible: The Jews for Judaism Counter-Missionary Survival Guide (Baltimore, Md.: 2004), 4-5, www.jewsforjudaism.org/web/byg/pdf/ J4J_CMSGW16.pdf. For references to repentance, see 2 Chronicles 7:14; Ezekiel 18 and 33; Jeremiah 36:3; Isaiah 55:6-7; and Jonah 3:10.

130 Matthew 3:2.

131 Luke 5:32.

132 See Mark 6:7-13.

133 Emphasis added.

134 See 1 Samuel 15:22.

135 For an early example, see Acts 8:26-39.

136 Isaiah 1:4.

137 See Psalm 44.

138 Isaiah 53:2.

139 See John 1:46.

140 See Matthew 21:13. The term "den of robbers" was a reference to Jeremiah 7:11—"Has this house, which bears my Name, become a den of robbers to you?"

141 See Acts 8:26-39.

142 See Matthew 5:39.

143 "He shall see his seed..." Isaiah 53:10 (KJV).

144 See Isaiah 1:4 (KJV). Isaiah also called Israel "a seed of evildoers" in Isaiah 14:20 (KJV) and "a seed of falsehood" in Isaiah 57:4 (KJV).

145 Seed can mean: "As marked by moral quality = persons (or community) of such a quality." See: Francis Brown, S. Driver, and C. Briggs, *The Brown-Driver-Briggs Hebrew and English Lexicon* (New York: Oxford University Press, 1959), 283.

146 For the story of Louis S. Lapides, who was raised in a Jewish home but became a follower of Jesus largely based on Isaiah 53, see Strobel, *The Case for Christ*, 171-87. Lapides is now the pastor of a California church and is the former president of a national network of messianic congregations.

147 See Charles A. Briggs, *Messianic Prophecy* (New York: Scribner's, 1889), 326, quoted in Kaiser, *The Messiah in the Old Testament*, 112-13.

148 See Tovia Singer, "Judaism's Response to Christian Missionaries," www.outreachjudaism.org/like-a-lion.html (Dec. 27, 2006).

149 See William G. Braude, Pesikta Rabbati: *Homiletical Discourses for Festal Days and Special Sabbaths*, 2 vols. (New Haven, Conn.: Yale, 1968), 680-87.

150 See Robert Kittel, *Theologians under Hitler* (New Haven, Conn.: Yale, 1985).

151 See Edward H. Flannery, *The Anguish of the Jews: Twenty-Three Centuries of Anti-Semitism* (New York: Paulist, 1985).

Challenge #6

152 Wendi's story and her quotes are from: David Ian Miller, "Finding My Religion," www.sfgate.com/cgi-bin/article.cgi?file=/g/a/2006/07/24/findrelig.DTL (Jan. 12, 2007).

153 "Mixing Religious Teachings," CBS Poll (June 29, 2005), www.cbsnews.com/stories/2005/06/29/opinion/polls/main705181.shtml (Jan. 4, 2007).

154 James R. Edwards, *Is Jesus the Only Savior?* (Grand Rapids, Mich.: Eerdmans, 2005), 5.

155 See John 18:38.

156 See Romans 2:14-15.

157 Cited in C. S. Lewis, ed., *George MacDonald: An Anthology* (New York: Macmillan, 1978), 7.

158 Hebrews 9:27—"Man is destined to die once, and after that to face judgment..."

159 For a discussion of the topic "A Loving God Would Never Torture People in Hell," see Strobel, *The Case for Faith*, 169-94.

160 Shirley MacLaine, *Out on a Limb* (New York: Bantam, 1983), 347.

161 Revised Standard Version.

162 See Matthew 7:1-5.

163 "Straightening the Record: Some Response to Critics," *Modern Theology* 6 (Jan. 1990), 187.

164 John Shelby Spong, *Why Christianity Must Change or Die* (San Francisco: HarperSanFrancisco, 1999), 95.

165 Edwards, *Is Jesus the Only Savior?* 151.

166 Romans 6:23—"For the wages of sin is death, but the gift of God is eternal life in Christ Jesus our Lord."

167 See John 10:11-18.

168 Dan Kimball, *They Like Jesus but Not the Church* (Grand Rapids, Mich.: Zondervan, 2007), 30.

169 Cathleen Falsani, *The God Factor* (New York: Sarah Crichton, 2006), 9.

170 See Hebrews 10:24-25.

Conclusion

171 See Galatians 5:22-23.

172 All quotes from Anne Rice are from: Anne Rice, *Author's Note in Christ the Lord: Out of Egypt* (New York: Knopf, 2005), 305-22.

173 C. S. Lewis, *Mere Christianity* (New York: HarperCollins, revised and amplified edition, 2001), 196-97.

174 Three verses from the New Testament book of Romans are often used to sum up the gospel: Romans 3:23—"For all have sinned and fall short of the glory of God."